BEST
GREEN
EATS
EVER

DELICIOUS RECIPES FOR NUTRIENT-RICH LEAFY GREENS, HIGH IN ANTIOXIDANTS AND MORE

Katrine van Wyk

Foreword by Frank Lipman, M.D.

Published by The Countryman Press, P.O. Box 748, Woodstock, VT 05091

Distributed by W. W. Norton & Company, Inc., 500 Fifth Avenue, New York, NY 10110

Printed in the United States

Best Green East Ever
ISBN 978-1-58157-287-2

10 9 8 7 6 5 4 3 2 1

Unless otherwise indicated, all photography courtesy of the author.

Page 2, 11, 13, 16, 17, 25, 53, 55, 61, 62, 77, 78, 94, 97, 113, 115, 116, 117, 120, 122, 123, 124, 127, 138, 145, 152, 153, 156, 157, 162, 163, 169, 171, 180, 190, 191, 199, 202, 203, 209, 210: © Patryce Bak; 7: © 8thCreator/iStockphoto.com; 8, 23: © robynmac/iStockphoto.com; 9: © GMEVIPHOTO/ shutterstock.com; 18: © Lighthousebay/iStockphoto.com; 21: © robynmac /iStockphoto.com; 22: © simonbradfield/iStockphoto.com; 27: © ninikas/iStockphoto.com; 29: © Skystorm/ iStockphoto.com, © Matt_Gibson/iStockphoto.com, © THEPALMER/iStockphoto.com; 31: © beba2304/iStockphoto.com, © vm/iStockphoto.com, © ehaurylik/iStockphoto.com; 33: © GomezDavid/iStockphoto.com, © jeehyun/iStockphoto.com, © NevaF/iStockphoto.com; 35: © -Ivinst-/iStockphoto.com; 37: © destigter-photo/iStockphoto.com, © Olha_Alfanasieva/ iStockphoto.com, © PicLeidenschaft/iStockphoto.com; 43: © Even André Rygg; 44: © eskymaks/iStockphoto.com, 45: © fotografiche/iStockphoto.com; 46: © jrwasserman/ iStockphoto.com; 47: © kcline/iStockphoto.com; 48: © stuartbur/iStockphoto.com; 49: © phototropic/iStockphoto.com; 50: © chrisgramly/iStockphoto.com; 51: © rudisill/iStockphoto. com; 56, 57: © cmillc22/iStockphoto.com; 58, 59: © mllevphoto/iStockphoto.com; 67: © YingYang/iStockphoto.com; 69: © Wiktory/iStockphoto.com; 70: © bit245/iStockphoto. com; 73: © Maria_Lapina/iStockphoto.com; 74, 75: © cobraphoto/iStockphoto.com; 81: © enzodebernardo/iStockphoto.com; 82, 83: © Lesya Dolyuk/Shutterstock.com; 87: © drewhadley/ iStockphoto.com; 89: © katerinabelaya/iStockphoto.com; 91: © kajakiki/iStockphoto.com; 98: © pushlama/iStockphoto.com; 101: © MonaMakela/iStockphoto.com; 102: © ballycroy/iStockphoto. com; 108, 109, 146: © bhofack2/iStockphoto.com 110, 111: © rjgrant/iStockphoto.com; 129: © nata_vkusidey/iStockphoto.com; 130: © sf_foodphoto/iStockphoto.com; 133: © MarcQuebec/ iStockphoto.com; 134: © Anna Hoychuk/Shutterstock.com; 143: © SandraKim/iStockphoto. com; 149: © TheCrimsonMonkey/iStockphoto.com; 150: © magnez2/iStockphoto.com; 161: © bjones27/iStockphoto.com; 164, 165: © georgeblomfield/iStockphoto.com; 175: © TeQuiO/ iStockphoto.com; 177: © Zoryanchik/iStockphoto.com; 179: © jimmychou/iStockphoto.com; 185: © kimeveruss/iStockphoto.com; 193: © ElenaGaak/shutterstock.com;

Cover: © ElenaGaak/shutterstock.com; © 8thCreator/iStockphoto.com; © robynmac/ iStockphoto.com; © Anna Hoychuk/Shutterstock.com; © Lesya Dolyuk/Shutterstock.com

BEST GREEN EATS EVER

For all of us who strive to do better

BEST GREEN EATS EVER
CONTENTS

Chapter 3: Sides / 107

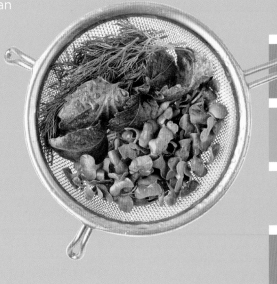

Chapter 4: Snacks & Sauces / 139

Chapter 5: Mains / 159

Chapter 6: Treats / 190

Wow, have things changed since I wrote my first book, *Best Green Drinks Ever*, just one year ago. I've become a mom and a published author. And I no longer have lots of time to hang out in my kitchen uninterrupted. This book is a result of that. In my new and full life as a mom, time is precious, and a healthy diet is vital for all of us to stay energized and sane, and for my little guy to grow big and strong.

This is how I cook. My dinner goal is always to get a delicious, nutritious meal on the table for my little family in as little time as possible, and try to have fun while doing it. That means keeping things simple, using fresh ingredients that require less "processing," and opting for cooking techniques that are fast. Cooking dinner in my house often involves chopping sweet potatoes while my son, Felix, pulls himself up on my pants (or pulls my pants off—either way) or swishing kale in my salad spinner while he's on the floor re-sorting our recycling and banging what has now become his measuring cups. Who needs fancy toys, right?

The recipes in this book are based on meals that I make every day. They are inspired by some of my favorite restaurants and health-food spots, my travels around the world, my endless hours spent reading food blogs and cookbooks (that was all before I became a mom), and, of course, my absolute love for all things green. From kale to avocados, I just can't get enough. What is this obsession with greens? You might ask. And rightfully so. Well, first of all, dark, leafy greens are some of the most nutrient-dense foods per calorie you can find. They are full of minerals, antioxidants, fiber, protein, and chlorophyll and generally make me feel awesome. They also help protect us from environmental damage, support our bodies' natural detox process (which we all need in this modern world), and even prevent cancer. But the reason for my obsession with greens goes beyond even that. Greens are the antidote to all the heavier, starchy, rich, and processed foods so many of us eat too much of. They bring something vibrant, uplifting, and bright to our plate. As opposed to white and processed foods, greens are fresh, living, and fibrous. If you're looking to find more energy and balance in your life (and who isn't?), add some greens to your plate.

As much as I wish it were different, America's vegetable consumption is not as good as it should be. The most commonly eaten vegetables include french fries and ketchup. Still. We need to do better. We know food and lifestyle play an enormous role in preventing diseases and ailments of all kinds. We know that food can be our medicine. We know the choices we make every day matter. So let's do something about this and start taking better care of our bodies. I hope this book—with its accessible recipes, vibrant photos, and un-fussy fun—will ignite something in you and maybe even inspire you to pick up a bunch of leafy, green goodness and eat it. And when you start eating better, maybe your coworkers will start asking what you're so smiley about, or why your skin is glowing, or how you lost those last pounds. And you'll tell them why. And then they'll start eating their greens, too. Simple as that.

—Katrine van Wyk

Greens, greens, and more greens! From spinach to kale, Brussels sprouts to collards, leafy greens are appearing in all sorts of unexpected places. It has never been easier to pump up your meals with a great big healthy green punch. You can find them in your grocery store aisles, at farmer's markets, even sometimes in your own backyard garden. Regardless of where you buy them, greens are just delicious and right anytime of the day or night.

As a doctor, I'm passionate about "good medicine." This means I'm not just interesting in treating illnesses as they arise but also in preventing them through a whole host of complementary strategies. I'm a firm believer that making healthy choices at mealtimes is one of the easiest and best ways to help maintain a healthy lifestyle. Katrine's BEST GREEN EATS EVER is a great first step to beginning—and maintaining—optimum health.

I know Katrine well, as she works as a Holistic Health Coach in my practice. Patients love her calm and perceptive demeanor, and the nutritional guidance she provides. In her first book, BEST GREEN DRINKS EVER, she gave us an exciting new crop of green juice recipes. Now, I'm thrilled to be a part of her latest project BEST GREEN EATS EVER that takes readers beyond the blender and into the world of delicious, healthy, and filling meals and snacks for every occasion. After all, we cannot live on juice alone! These new recipes reflect Katrine's dedication to creating meals that are both healthy and tasty.

By now we're all aware that we should be including more leafy green veggies in our diets. Kale is a superfood packed with vitamin A; spinach is loaded with antioxidant flavonoids, potassium, and vitamin B6; and Brussels sprouts have a ton of vitamin C. They are the most nutritionally dense foods available. The benefits are endless. Which is why BEST GREEN EATS EVER is such an exciting new addition to my bookshelf. Quick, easy, and delicious recipes that nourish the body from the inside out—now that's the kind of "medicine" that's easy to swallow.

Katrine's recipes use some of my favorite greens in new and tasty ways. Try her Shredded Chicken and Savoy Cabbage for a protein-packed lunch on the go or dish up some Brussels Sprouts Chips (really!) for a midday snack that will have your family asking for more. Of course, Katrine also includes some classic dishes too, like her Grilled Caesar Salad that will leave you feeling energized, not weighed down. She's also included modifications for nearly every diet including gluten-free, paleo, raw, and vegan—so everyone can enjoy the benefits of these great green eats.

At the Eleven Eleven Wellness Center, we encourage our patients to become proactive in their own health and partner with them as they journey towards true health and optimal wellness. With her latest book, Katrine van Wyk helps guide her readers to good health.

—Dr. Frank Lipman

A pioneer and internationally recognized expert in the fields of Integrative and Functional Medicine, Dr. Frank Lipman is the founder and director of Eleven Eleven Wellness Center in New York City, where his personal brand of healing has helped thousands of people reclaim their vitality and recover their zest for life.

WHY EAT GREENS?

We all know we should eat plenty of vegetables. It's probably one of those things you can hear your mother's voice repeating in your head, but what exactly is so special about the green ones? Many of us grew up to hate them. Broccoli, brussels sprouts, and cabbage were considered bland, boring, watered-down "health food" that parents had to use every negotiation trick they had to make you eat. Often they were simply boiled or steamed and served as an overcooked mush. There was no excitement or enjoyment associated with them. What a shame! These green goodies are, yes, loaded with nutrients, but they are also lip-smacking delicious when handled with some TLC. Now that I'm a mother myself and cooking dinner for my family every day, I've made it my mission to make these greens a delicious, enjoyable, and daily part of our plates.

So back to the nutrients. What's actually in these greens?

First, dark, leafy greens are some of the most nutrient-dense plant foods around. These include kale, spinach, Swiss chard, and collard greens, which are packed with antioxidants, vitamins A and C, and minerals such as iron, calcium, and folic acid. Anyone worried about getting enough iron in their diet (hello, mammas!) should turn to leafy greens. A serving of beet greens contains about the same amount of iron as a small steak. For all of us who don't drink cow's milk, one cup of spinach contains close to the same amount of calcium as a cup of milk.

If that isn't enough to whet your appetite, the beta-carotene found in these greens does wonders for your skin and is believed to be an important antioxidant that prevents cancer. Leafy greens are also great for your bones because of both the high levels of calcium, magnesium, and potassium they contain and the fact that they are alkaline and therefore do not cause urinary calcium loss.

All leafy greens are also packed with fiber, which helps slow the rise of blood sugar after you eat, keeping you feeling full and satisfied for longer and helping lower blood cholesterol. Fiber is also crucial for the body's ability to eliminate toxins. It helps minimize our exposure to toxins that can enter our bodies through our food and to chemicals that can damage our DNA.

The Anticancer Food: Cruciferous Vegetables

The vegetables in what's called the Brassica family, referred to as cruciferous vegetables, have been shown again and again to have great cancer-preventing benefits. They are packed with micronutrients and antioxidants and may just be the world's most healthy vegetables. Green cruciferous vegetables include kale, spinach, bok choy, cabbage, broccoli, brussels sprouts, and collard greens.

While these foods are incredibly nutritious and delicious, I should also mention that they do contain a few so-called anti-nutrients—this is an issue that comes up in the press from time to time, scaring many people unnecessarily. So I'd like to take the bull by the horns and address this straight on: It has been shown that, when consumed RAW and in HIGH QUANTITIES, these vegetables may cause some thyroid issues and even lead to kidney stones. Glucosinolates are compounds that, in large quantities, *may* inhibit iodine uptake, resulting eventually in hypothyroidism and promoting goiter formation (glucosinolates are sometimes referred to as goitrogens). Cruciferous vegetables also contain oxalates, which can promote kidney stones—again only when eaten raw and in large quantities.

As long as you don't overdo it with lots of uncooked dishes and drinks, you should be just fine. If you already have a thyroid condition or are at all worried about this (maybe you've overdone it with raw foods for a while), stick to more of the cooked recipes and limit your intake of raw cruciferous vegetables to four servings a week—that still allows you to start most of your days with a green smoothie or have a delicious spinach salad for lunch.

There are also plenty of green, healthy vegetables that do not contain these compounds, including most lettuces, asparagus, zucchini, green beans, celery, cucumber, and peas. The most important thing is that you start to eat more whole un-processed foods (think roast chicken instead of chicken nuggets), including lots of plants and healthy fats, and get cooking. That will all contribute to making you an even healthier person, full of energy and vitality.

The Energetics of Foods and Greens

The energetics of food has to do with how the food functions and sees that a function in the plant is mirrored in us. For example, a turnip is a root vegetable that grows under ground, in dark soil – and to us turnips have a grounding effect, helping us stay calm, focused and down to earth. Leafy greens, as opposed to root vegetables, grow upward and outward. They spread their leaves and reach up toward the sky to catch as much sunlight as they can. The idea is that this energy is transferred to us when we eat them—that leafy greens have an uplifting, light, and energizing effect on us. One is not better than the other, and we certainly need both to stay balanced.

Someone who is feeling a bit sluggish, tired, and heavy would likely benefit from adding more leafy greens to their diet. And vice versa—someone feeling a bit anxious or restless would probably do well with some more root vegetables.

Think about this: During photosynthesis, green leaves take in carbon dioxide and give off oxygen. Their function is similar to that of human lungs, although in reverse—we take in oxygen and expel carbon dioxide. Just look at a big kale leaf—it actually looks like a human lung. Leafy greens do wonders for our respiratory system, helping to clear out mucus and because these plants contain chlorophyll, they also help supply our blood with oxygen.

I am fascinated with eastern approaches to food, cooking, medicine, and health. Both Chinese medicine and Ayurveda take an individualized approach; neither advocates that one diet is right for everyone. Instead, they take into account your body type, constitution, and any imbalances that are present before "prescribing" foods, tools, and herbs to help you regain optimal balance.

Chinese Medicine

In Chinese medicine, nutrition and food are viewed a bit differently than in Western medicine. It's the *quality* of the food that's in focus, and what determines whether a food is beneficial is its effect on the human body, not just the grams of each micronutrient it contains. I love viewing food this way. It makes so much more sense to look at a food as a whole, where all the nutrients play together—*with* our bodies—to give us the optimal benefits. Foods are described by their qualities: temperature, flavor, and action. For example, kale would be described as purifying, warming, and strengthening for the stomach. It's said to be able to stop pain and has been used for stopping stomach ulcers.

Ayurveda

Ayurveda is a five-thousand-year-old system of natural healing. It originates from the Vedic culture of India; Chinese Medicine actually has its roots in Ayurveda. According to this system, health is the balanced and dynamic integration between our environment, body, mind, and spirit. The approach is to identify an individual's ideal state and then offer tools such as diet, bodywork, and meditation.

According to Ayurveda, a balanced meal should include all six flavors— sweet, spicy, salty, bitter, pungent, and astringent—to ensure that we feel balanced and satisfied. Leafy greens are described as bitter, a flavor many of us might avoid or simply just not eat enough of. We tend to eat way too many sweet and salty foods.

Bitter foods also include green and yellow vegetables, celery, broccoli, sprouts, and beets, and they are described as detoxifying to the system.

Which Greens Do What?

A general rule for the nutritional benefits of lettuce goes from dark to light—the darker the leaf, the more nutritious it is. In the next few pages, I'll review the various choices, broken down into the following groups:

THE SCIENCE OF GREENS

Modern science has certainly proven our ancestors were right about leafy greens being nutrient powerhouses and confirmed that these vegetables are indeed among the most nutrient-dense foods on the planet. With modern science's ability to pick apart and measure the exact quantity of each nutrient found in a food, they've found that leafy greens are high in vitamin A and C, beta-carotene, folic-acid, calcium and chlorophyll, just to name a few!

1. LETTUCES

Lettuces are primarily water and extremely low in calories, which is why they are also a common diet food. Although they are not the most nutritious greens out there, they are still a great and healthy food.

2. DARK, LEAFY GREENS

Dark, leafy greens are the true powerhouses of the plant world, rich in minerals such as calcium, iron, and magnesium and loaded with the vital antioxidants that help our cells combat environmental stressors and toxins. These beauties help support the cardiovascular system, are loaded with fiber, and are anti-inflammatory.

Some of my favorites are listed below.

3. CRUCIFEROUS GREENS

Cabbage is often referred to as the king of the cruciferous vegetables, and all the different cabbages have similar nutritional benefits. They are all full of fiber, which is good for our digestion and helps feed our gut bacteria. They are also celebrated for their anticancer benefits, as they contain more phytochemicals with anticancer properties than any other vegetable. These phytochemicals both increase the antioxidant defense mechanism in the body and help with detoxification of chemicals and hormones. Cabbages are also rich in vitamins C and B6, biotin, potassium, and folic acid, among others. Other cruciferous vegetables are broccoli, broccolini, and broccoli rabe.

4. WILD GREENS

Foraging for greens has gotten popular, and for good reason. You can often find "weeds" in your backyard—or cultivated and sold at a farmer's market—that are extremely healthy. The right plants aren't just weeds, but also nourishing and healing herbs. Often, the whole plant can be used—flower, leaves, and roots—but be careful to make sure you know what you're picking and eating. I talk about two very common wild greens.

5. HERBS

Herbs are generally also leafy and green, so I thought they deserved a place here, too. Herbs are aromatic plants and have long been used as digestants, which aid in the digestive process and help relieve digestive discomfort. Adding fresh and dried herbs to your meals is the fastest, easiest, and healthiest way to increase flavor, variety, and nutrients. If you're concerned about eating too much salt, sugar, and other additives, make friends with these.

LETTUCES

arugula (a.k.a. rucola)

Arugula is a great source of folic acid and vitamins A, C, and K. As one of the best vegetable sources of vitamin K, it provides a boost for bone and brain health. It has a spicy, peppery taste and is delicious on its own with a little olive oil and lemon juice.

boston and bibb (butterhead)

Butterhead lettuces have soft, large, and buttery leaves that are great as "cups" for different fillings. In Asian cooking they often get used in that way as vehicles for meats, herbs, and dipping sauces. Or tossed with a simple vinaigrette, they make the perfect side salad. They are quite easy to grow yourself or find at your local farmers market in the spring and summer.

escarole

Escarole is a curly lettuce and a winter green with a nice bitter flavor. It's great as a salad on its own or mixed with milder lettuces.

iceberg

Iceberg is probably the most common lettuce of all, although not the most nutritious. It has a great crunchy texture and a very mild flavor that needs a bit of dressing and love to be elevated to deliciousness (no wonder blue cheese is a common partner for the iceberg lettuce wedge).

romaine

Romaine lettuce is probably the most nutrient-dense lettuce. It is high in vitamins A, C, B1, and B2. It also contains folic acid, calcium, and quite a bit of protein (around 7 grams per head). It even contains some omega-3 fatty acids. Romaine is a great lettuce for salads and really great for juicing and in green smoothies. Did you know you can even throw it on the grill? (See page 92 for a recipe.)

DARK, LEAFY GREENS

collard greens

Collards' large leaves are a staple in Southern cooking, usually accompanied by some porky goodness. The large leaves are versatile, nutrient-dense, and great both cooked and raw. I love using them as wraps.

kale

Kale is all the rage today, but it's far from a new food. It was one of the most common green vegetables eaten until the end of the Middle Ages; the curly leafed ancestor of kale was prevalent in Greece in the fourth century B.C. Kale contains compounds (glucosinolate and cysteine sulfoxide) that can help switch on the detox enzymes in the liver.

mustard greens

Mustard greens are in fact the leaves of the mustard plant (its seeds are used to make mustard). These spring greens are another member of the cruciferous or brassica family. As with the other family members, they're celebrated for their anticancer benefits due to their big load of antioxidants, and they are rich in bone-strengthening minerals such as calcium, magnesium, and folic acid.

spinach

Spinach comes in a few different shapes and sizes—curly leaves, flat leaves, large bunches, or baby leaves. The smaller, younger spinach has a mild flavor and is delicious in smoothies and raw salads. The large curly spinach lends itself better to cooking and sautéing. But whichever kind you get and like, it's all good for you, packed with minerals, vitamin C, and other antioxidants.

swiss chard

Swiss chard is a nutrient powerhouse and a relative of the beet plant. With large green leaves and red, yellow, purple, or white stems, it's a beautiful plant to cook with. Like kale and the other dark, leafy greens, it's packed with vitamins C, A, and K and minerals such as magnesium, calcium, and iron.

CRUCIFEROUS GREENS

bok choy

You've probably had bok choy at an Asian restaurant of some kind. It's delicious stir fried and baby bok choy can be prepared and served whole, which makes a pretty side dish.

broccoli, broccolini, and broccoli rabe

Broccoli, broccolini, and broccoli rabe are tree-like green vegetables of different textures and flavors. With soft, floral florets and heartier, more bitter stems, they are a fun feast. These also are anticancer foods, and rich in vitamin C and minerals. While broccoli is the most commonly used and found version, you'll also see the thinner broccolini, a mix of broccoli and kale. Broccoli rabe (also called rapini) has more green leaves and does not form large florets; it has a much stronger pungent flavor.

brussels sprouts

Did you know that brussels sprouts grow on a stick under ground? These mini-cabbages were developed from wild cabbages, and the first mention of the delicious little heads was in Brussels, Belgium, in the 1500s. Nutritionally, this is another anticancer powerhouse and a great source of vitamin C, folic acid, and fiber.

green cabbage

Green cabbage is the classic cabbage, most commonly used in coleslaws, soups, and stews. Cabbage is also a good source of the amino acid glutamine which is a critical player in the growth and regeneration of the cells that line the gastrointestinal tract. Glutamine is also believed to help curb sugar cravings!

napa or chinese cabbage

The napa variety is the oblong-shaped cabbage with the white bottom half and light green, curly leaves. It's got a mildly bitter taste and a nice crispy texture that is great in salads and stir-fries.

savoy cabbage

The savoy is a darker green cabbage with curly and slightly softer leaves. The leaves are actually quite tender and soft even when raw, so this is a great cabbage for slaws, salads, and wraps.

WILD GREENS

Dandelion

The dandelion's green leaves are loaded with vitamin C and carotenoid, an antioxidant. In addition to its high nutrient content, dandelion contains compounds that improve liver function and other medicinal compounds that help tone the whole body. This is one very potent plant.

Although this plant grows in the wild, and probably on your lawn, it is also cultivated and available at natural food stores, farmers markets, and some supermarkets. If you are going to pick your own, early spring is the best time to do so, before the stem grows and the plant becomes tougher and more bitter.

Purslane

Purslane is a succulent plant that many may think of as just a weed. It has small thick leaves and a reddish stem. It also has the highest omega-3 levels of any green plant and is a delicious addition to summer salads.

HERBS

basil

Basil is a classic herb used in Italian cooking and the star of the much-loved pesto. It's also the perfect herb to combine with tomatoes. Basil is a digestive aid and can help treat a headache. It's also rich in anticancer antioxidants, and sweet basil even has antibacterial benefits.

cilantro (coriander)

Cilantro is an exotic-tasting herb that people tend to either love or hate. I happen to love it, so you'll see it show up in a couple of dishes in this book. It's rich in minerals and can help prevent hypertension and anxiety and promote peaceful sleep. Maybe most fascinating of all is cilantro's ability to chelate heavy metals out of the body. It is, therefore, a great detoxing food that in our modern society is a good idea to consume regularly.

mint

Mint is a familiar herb to the mojito lovers among us and is also a common herb used for tea. There are twenty-five different kinds of mint, including spearmint and the most commonly used in cooking: peppermint. Mint has a naturally cooling and calming effect on both the body and the mind and is toning to the stomach. It can help relieve digestive problems and relax muscles. It's a natural chillpill.

parsley

Parsley is a long celebrated herb and certainly worth more space on our plates than it gets as a garnish. It's high in vitamin C and other antioxidants that can boost immunity and help prevent cancer. It's known as a nerve stimulant and can help improve energy level. So if you're feeling a little sluggish—bring out the parsley.

Local, Seasonal, and Organic: What's What and Does It Matter?

I covered the subject of local, seasonal, and organic foods in my first book, *Best Green Drinks Ever*, and I feel the information is worth repeating here. I am a fan of using local and seasonal foods and choosing organic over conventional whenever I can (I know it's not always possible). The benefits of seasonal fruits and vegetables are numerous.

Flavor

Produce that has been allowed to fully ripen in the sun tastes amazing. Freshly picked produce has the optimal characteristics—crispy, fragrant, juicy, and colorful. For example, summer heirloom tomatoes make all other tomatoes seem inferior. You can eat them like apples—raw, warm from the sun, and straight from the vine.

Nutrition

Plants get their nourishment from the sun and the soil. Seasonally fresh produce is picked when it is ripe and fully developed. Such a plant will have had more sun exposure, which means it will have higher levels of antioxidants.Studies have found that the levels of iodine and beta-carotene in milk are higher in the summer than in the winter months—ice cream, anyone?

Economy

It's simply a question of supply and demand. When there's abundance of a product, such as watermelons in the summer, the prices go down. Seasonal food is much cheaper to produce for the farmers, who would rather sell their products for a lower price than not at all. Cash in on the seasonal bounty.

Environment

Seasonal produce can grow without much added human assistance—for example, pesticides and genetic modification. We know how the toxic compounds in pesticides and insecticides can contaminate water, soil, and also our health. Seasonal food is more likely to be locally produced, as well, which reduces the load on our environment from transport, thus reducing the carbon footprint of the food.

Community

Getting to know where our food is coming from, who is growing our food, and how they do it makes us feel more connected to that whole process.

Community-supported agriculture (a.k.a. CSA) and farmers markets create communities around food that encourage us all to share our knowledge, ask questions, and engage in our own local environment. Together we are more powerful and can create big change.

Home Cooking

Eating seasonally also encourages us to cook more—and there really is nothing better we can do for our health. When you start to take back control of what you put into your body—which oil you choose to cook with, how much sugar you add to your food, and so forth—you are consciously making better, healthier choices for yourself. Cooking is a great activity to do with your whole family and your friends. What better way to show your love than with a home-cooked meal?

Creativity and Variety

Whether you shop at the market or you're part of a CSA, eating seasonally will keep challenging your creativity to come up with new, fun, and delicious dishes, based on what you find. Maybe you choose to search for a recipe online, look through some cookbooks, or go on sites like Pinterest to find new inspiration and ideas about what to do with all that kale (I'm obsessed with it, and you can find me there and follow my boards). Variety is also good for our bodies; by changing our menu according to what's available seasonally, we are less likely to develop food intolerances.

Support of Your Seasonal Needs

The natural cycle of produce is perfectly designed to support our health. Apples grow in the fall, and they are the perfect transition food, helping the body get rid of excess heat and cool down before winter. In the spring the abundance of leafy greens helps us alkalize, detox, and lose extra pounds after a long winter of heavier foods. In the summer we need to cool down and stay hydrated by eating more juicy fruits, antioxidant-rich berries, and hydrating cucumber and watermelon. Building a lifestyle around seasonal food facilitates the body's natural healing process.

Organic Benefits

Food grown outside of its season or natural environment needs a lot more human assistance, in the form of pesticides, waxes, chemicals, and preservatives, to grow and look appealing to us as consumers. By opting for local and seasonal food, we are more likely to get a cleaner product. Many small family farms cannot afford to go through the organic certification process but nevertheless follow natural and sustainable growing practices. So, when you shop at the farmers market, you don't have to be as careful about finding organic-labeled produce as when you shop at the supermarket.

Living in Harmony

Living in tune with nature's rhythms makes us more aware and appreciative of the beauty around us. We can choose to live in balance with our surroundings instead of constantly butting up against and living in conflict with nature. Embracing the natural rhythm of things also helps simplify our lives. Our options are limited, and we can trust that our food is nourishing and good for us.

Where to Buy Local Foods

Your local farmers market is the easiest and best place to buy fresh, local produce. You can buy your fruits, vegetables, eggs, and dairy straight from the farmer—without any middlemen. That means every penny you spend goes straight to supporting the farms in your area. It's a win-win situation. To find farmers markets in your area, you can use nfmd.org, or if you happen to live in New York City like me, try grownyc.org.

Another great way to get hold of great, local products is to join a CSA. Community-supported agriculture means that you pay a share at the beginning of the season and then you will pick up a box of freshly picked produce once (or sometimes several times) a week. Many CSAs have multiple pick-up locations, so that you can find one convenient to you. If you live near a farm or farming community, the pick-up might be on the farm itself. The exciting aspect of a CSA box is that you never know exactly what will be in it each week, which may give you a little push to try new foods and be creative in using what you get. Other CSAs actually let you pick and choose and put together your own box of goodies. A CSA tends to be best suited for people who enjoy cooking and experimenting a little.

If you're lucky enough to live near a co-op or independent health food store, chances are they carry a variety of local and organic produce, in addition to some imported foods. Shopping at such a place may allow you to get the variety you're used to but with lots of great seasonal options to add to your shopping basket. This can be a bit more convenient, as you can often find everything you need in one place. Many supermarkets—and, of course, Whole Foods Markets—are starting to incorporate more local and organic food options. Thankfully, it has become a bit trendy at the moment, so let's take advantage of that and keep the momentum going.

Setting Up Your Kitchen for Success

To make cooking fun, easy, and seamless, you need to set up your kitchen for success. You don't need a lot of fancy gadgets and tools. Instead, you need a clean working space, some easy, reachable basics, and some pantry staples handy to get you cooking in no time.

ESSENTIAL TOOLS

- Knives. Get at least one big, sharp knife. It's super versatile and can be used for chopping vegetables, carving meat, or slicing fish.

- Wooden or bamboo mixing spoons.

- Tongs. They make tossing and turning food a breeze. Use for tossing salads together, mixing and sautéing vegetables, cooking meat, and turning meat or vegetables on the barbeque.

- Wooden cutting board. Forget about plastic! It's not good for you or the planet.

- Glass storage containers. They are easy to clean, pretty to look at, and see-through, so you'll know exactly what's inside them. Most important, they are safe, free of BPA and other plastic nasties.

- Salad spinner. Washes all your leafy greens, herbs, and smaller vegetables and spins them dry. Makes cooking so much easier. Trust me.

- A few mixing bowls. I like stainless steel, glass, or ceramic. One big and one small should do the trick.

- Measuring cups and spoons. They double as toys for any toddler.

- Salad bowl. To serve all your salads in, of course.

- Container or immersion blender. One or the other—or both. I love and use my high-power blender a lot, but it's an investment, as the good ones tend to be pricey. A smaller blender or an immersion blender will be fine for most sauces and soups. If you also have a food processer, you'll be more than fine.

- Grater. Get a fine one that works for ginger, garlic, and lemon zest.

- A few ovenproof baking dishes. I like the glass ones, and they are affordable and easy to find. One large and a smaller one should do.

- Cast-iron skillet. You can cook pretty much anything in it—and it's safe to put in the oven.

- A few stainless-steel or ceramic pots for cooking and steaming.

- Steam basket

- Strainer

- Pepper grinder

Stocking Up

COOKING OILS AND FATS

Fat helps with the absorption of nutrients from the greens, so skip the fat-free dressings and pour on the good stuff. This list tells you which fats and oils are best to use, and when to use them.

- *Olive oil.* Olive oil has been a staple in the Mediterranean diet and is now in the rest of the western world, too. It's a great oil for salad dressings, drizzling, and cooking meats or veggies over low or medium heat. Olive oil has a smoke point of 375°F, so generally try not to heat it above that. I use olive oil to roast vegetables and make kale chips in this book.
  - **What to buy:** Always buy organic olive oil in a dark glass bottle. If you are using it to flavor food, to drizzle over your vegetables, for example, spend a little more money on a fragrant, delicious oil.

- *Butter.* That's right. Butter is on my list of very healthy fats. But it should be from grass-fed cows. Because the cow was eating grass, the butter contains omega-3 fatty acids; and because the cow was allowed to be outside in the sun, the butter contains vitamin D. Butter from grass-fed cows is also a good source of vitamin K, a vitamin many of us don't get enough of. Butter is best used after cooking as a spread, dip, or dollop, because it has a smoke point of 300°F. If you're sautéing over low heat, butter is fine for cooking.
  - **What to buy:** Organic or grass-fed butter is always the way to go. You want to avoid conventional butter from cows fed a diet full of hormones and antibiotics. It's not a good life for the cows, and those toxins are not good for our bodies.

- *Ghee.* Ghee, like butter, is derived from cow's milk. It's basically clarified butter and therefore contains no casein, a protein found in cow's milk that some people are sensitive to. Ghee has been used in India for ages and is a great fat for cooking due to its high smoke point. It has a balanced ratio of omega-6 and omega-3 fatty acids, something that is important because today most of us eat too much food with only omega-6 fatty acids.

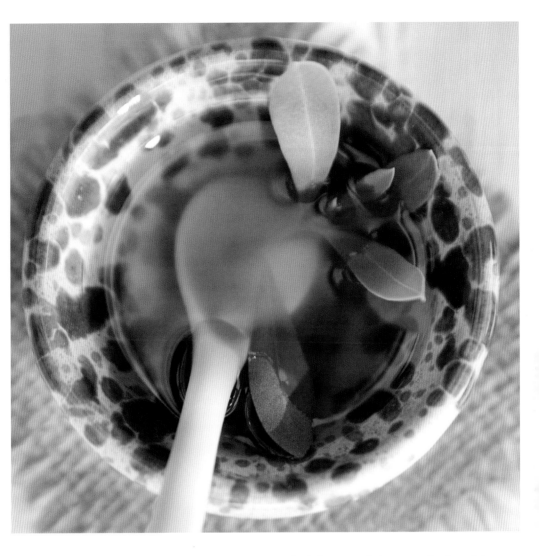

- **What to buy:** As with butter, you want to look for grass-fed or organic ghee. It is also possible to make your own ghee from butter. Just look it up.

- *Coconut oil.* Coconut oil is my favorite fat, and I use it for more than just cooking. It's my makeup remover, body lotion, and baby oil for my little one. It has a delicious, exotic scent and adds a little nutty sweetness to foods. It's great for roasting root vegetables and sautéing greens and works well in baking, too.

  - **What to buy:** Look for raw, unprocessed or unrefined coconut oil. You may also see "virgin" or "cold pressed" on the label, and that's all good. And organic is always a superior choice.

- *Other nut or seed oils.* Pumpkin seed oil, walnut oil, and toasted sesame seed oil are example of flavoring oils that should only be used cold, drizzled on the food after cooking to add delicious flavor.

  - **What to buy:** Again, just look for organic if you can find it and stick to pure oils.

FRIDGE AND PANTRY SUPPLIES

The following list provides some of the products that you should always have fresh or in the fridge:

- Garlic

- Onion

- Ginger

- Fresh parsley, cilantro, or basil

- Fresh lemon

- Kale, Swiss chard, or collard greens

- Head of lettuce or bag of lettuce mix

- A few root vegetables, sweet potato, or winter squash

- Grass-fed butter

- Almond butter

- Raw sauerkraut

In the pantry these ingredients are important to have on hand:

- Good salt (Real Salt, Himalayan sea salt, or Celtic sea salt)

- Whole black pepper

- A few dried herbs—for example, Italian blend, tarragon, turmeric, cumin, and curry

- Apple cider vinegar, my go-to vinegar for everything

- Gluten-free tamari, a fermented soy sauce alternative

- Coconut aminos, or fermented coconut sap—slightly sweet and salty and a soy-free alternative to soy sauce

- Umeboshi vinegar, a Japanese plum vinegar with a delicious, tart flavor

- Extra virgin olive oil—the go-to for simple sautés and salad dressings

- Toasted sesame seed oil—adds lots of flavor to simple stir-fries and sautés

- Coconut oil—for everything

- Ghee—can be added to your oatmeal—seriously!

- Your favorite seeds and nuts, including flax seeds and chia seeds

- Herbamare or other herbal salt alternatives—sometimes all that steamed vegetables need

- Dulse flakes—loaded with natural salty flavor and iodine

- Dried or canned beans—simple vegetarian protein option

- Lentils—quick to cook and simply delicious

- Gluten-free pasta—because we all crave a bowl of pasta from time to time. I like the brown rice and quinoa options

- Quinoa—a complete protein source that can be used a million different ways for breakfast, lunch, or dinner

- Buckwheat and 100% buckwheat noodles—lots of protein and fiber

- Any other gluten-free grains and seeds that you like, such as amaranth, pumpkin seeds, millet, coconut flour, almond flour, wild rice, and pine nuts

How to Properly Store Your Food

WHAT GOES IN THE FRIDGE?

Use the vegetable and fruit drawers in your fridge for exactly those items. They are built to keep the ideal temperature and moisture for your produce. Once you notice something starting to go off, get it out of there—or else it will speed up the spoiling of your other produce, too. Here's what goes in the fridge:

- Berries

- Leafy greens. Store in a perforated plastic bag or wrap the unwashed greens in damp paper towels and place in a plastic bag in the refrigerator's vegetable drawer. If stored properly, leafy greens should last five days in the fridge

- Most vegetables: root vegetables, zucchini, peppers, broccoli, cucumber, and celery

- All herbs (except basil) should be stored in the fridge, preferably in a glass of water or in a plastic bag with a damp paper towel wrapped around the stems. You can also wash the herbs and dry them well before storing them in a glass jar with the lid on. That way they can last a whole week

WHAT STAYS ON THE COUNTER?

Let these foods be nice ornaments in bowls and baskets in your kitchen to inspire cooking and healthy eating:

- Sweet potatoes, potatoes, and winter squash

- Citrus

- Tomatoes and basil

- Avocados

- Onions and garlic

- Bananas

- Other tropical fruit, such as mango, pineapple, and papaya, which can ripen on the counter and then be placed in the fridge.

HOW TO STORE LEFTOVERS

Once you've cut into your fruit or vegetable, always store it in the refrigerator, covered. Store your leftovers in reusable, machine-washable glass containers such as mason jars and Glassware. There are also great stainless-steel options on the market for packing your lunch or snacks, as they don't break. These are clean and safe options, free of BPA and other nasties. Better for you and for the planet. If you store something in plastic, make sure to let the food cool down first. Try to avoid storing anything acidic (lemonade, vinegar, tomato sauce, etc.) in plastic—the acid actually pulls the toxins in the plastic out of the container and into your food.

Let the Leftovers Sing

Leftovers are your friends! You may have felt overwhelmed and a bit guilty when you've cooked way too much for dinner or maybe even closed your eyes as you tossed out a whole pot of rice. Well, never again. Embrace the leftovers and let them shine in a new way the next day. If you live alone and prefer not to cook a whole meal from scratch every night, plan ahead to actually make too much and that way you'll have delicious meals for days. Here are some of my favorite tricks for reusing and repurposing leftovers.

BUILD A BOWL

Got some leftover grains (rice, quinoa, millet, etc.), some fish, and some kind of roasted vegetable? Well, build a bowl! Layer a nice bowl with grains or sautéed greens at the bottom and your protein and vegetables in little groupings on top. Or simply toss it all together if you prefer. When you don't have enough leftovers to make a filling meal, add an egg with a runny yolk on top or some hummus or half an avocado. Give the whole bowl a generous sprinkle of some fresh, chopped herbs and maybe some nuts or seeds, and add some tahini sauce, pesto, or simply a squirt of lemon and a drizzle of olive oil.

BUILD A SALAD

Same concept here as with the bowl, but instead you use leftover salad and top it with more raw and chopped vegetables. Tomatoes, cucumber, lentils, beans, bacon, cheese . . .Whatever you've got on hand that sounds delicious to you that day. And think about it, most leftovers can be used as salad toppings. Grilled chicken, salmon, quinoa, roasted vegetables, and boiled pasta are all delicious in salads. Toss with a vinaigrette or some apple cider vinegar and enjoy as an easy lunch.

WRAP IT UP

Use romaine or Boston lettuce as a wrapper instead of wheat wraps, taco shells, or bread. These lettuce wraps or cups can become little vehicles for your leftovers. Just add some chopped vegetables; leftover meat, beans, or lentils; and a dollop of a sauce or dip, and you've got a fun meal on your hands.

SALAD FOR DAYS

Raw kale salads can last for days, even when dressed, because kale is such a sturdy green that it won't wilt or go mushy and soggy like some lettuces do. So don't be scared to make some extra and bring it to work the next day for lunch.

ADD AN EGG OR TWO

Toss your leftover greens, meats, and vegetables into a frittata or omelet for a weekend brunch. No one needs to know it wasn't part of the plan all along.

ONE-POT MEALS, STIR-FRIES, CASSEROLES, AND PASTA DISHES

Try combining your leftovers with some fresh ingredients, garlic, and herbs. Just sauté it all together in a pan or toss it with boiled pasta or noodles. You can also try making them into an old-school casserole by placing them in an oven-proof dish, adding some cheese on top, and baking. The best part about one-pot meals is—well, there's only one pot to clean.

Forget About a One-Size-Fits-All Diet

Dieting is out—a healthy lifestyle is in! Got it? Okay, good. Gone are the days of calorie counting, bland "health foods," and ridiculous restrictions. Life is way too short for that. However, we all strive to be better. To improve. To feel our best. To perform even better. To have even more energy. And that's where a healthy, delicious, and fun lifestyle comes in. Because we're in it for the long haul.

But the world of food, nutrition, and wellness can be a bit confusing. That's because there's not one lifestyle, one diet, or one way of doing things that fits everyone. What's toxic to one person can be completely fine for someone else. And what's nourishing you might hurt someone else. Many things influence who we are and what nourishes us: our ancestry, the climate where we live, the weather today, our mood, our activity level, stress, environmental toxins, body type, allergies and sensitivities, injuries, and so on. So even though your best friend can eat yogurt every day and feel great, you may not be able to do that. Maybe you have a friend who loves to eat lots of raw foods, while those same foods make you feel bloated or jittery and cold. Some people can tolerate wheat in their diets, while it makes others ill.

To make it simple and approachable for as many of you as possible to eat delicious and nourishing food, in this book I try to focus on foods that are generally anti-inflammatory and without a lot of ingredients that people tend to be sensitive to, such as gluten, dairy, soy, and corn.

I have experimented with lots of different approaches to food and "diets" (I don't like that word), and I am evolving and changing and tweaking things all the time. One thing I know is that for my body, gluten is no good. So I generally cook gluten free, and therefore all the recipes in this book are free of gluten-containing grains and flours. But beyond that you'll find some dishes that contain dairy and some that don't, some with meat and fish, some made purely with plants, some with and some without grains. No matter what your current lifestyle and plate look like, I hope you will find some delicious dishes that fit your needs and desires.

Descriptions Explained

- *Vegetarian.* A vegetarian dish is free of any meat, including fish, chicken, beef, and pork. It may, however, contain dairy or eggs.

- *Vegan.* A vegan dish contains no animal products or by-products whatsoever. It's free of meat, dairy, eggs, and honey.

- *Paleo*. Paleo describes dishes that are free of any grains, legumes, or dairy. Paleo is a diet based on what is thought to be that of our ancestors, the hunter-gatherers who lived in Paleolithic times. Although some people are not convinced that we know what those people ate, most agree that their diet was mainly made up of vegetables, roots, starchy tubers, meat, eggs, nuts, and seeds.

- *GF or Gluten Free*. Gluten is protein found in a few grains, including wheat, barley, rye, and spelt. All the dishes in this book are gluten free.

PART TWO

GREEN RECIPES

soups

Comforting and warm or cooling and refreshing. Smooth as silk or full of textures. Sweet and creamy or savory and delicious. Soups offer more variety, flavor, and nutrition than many of us tend to appreciate. But there's a reason soups and broths have long been celebrated as truly healing and nourishing to the soul. The reason broths are so nutritious is that the boiling of bones or vegetables pulls the minerals out of the foods and into the broth, or stock. A blended soup is very easy to digest, giving the digestive system a little break, something it needs from time to time, especially when we're feeling under the weather, tired and sluggish.

A pot of soup can be a quick and easy meal or an elaborate concoction. The recipes in this chapter tend more toward the former and are easy to make in large batches and store or freeze for future easy weeknight dinners. Of course, they are also loaded with greens, as soups are the perfect vehicle for sneaking in those extra nourishing foods. I hope you find some treasures and new staples on the pages that follow.

zucchini basil soup

This is a delicious soup of summery ingredients that is great year-round. It's light enough to enjoy as a starter or a snack but tasty enough to satisfy as a meal in and of itself. The arugula adds a nice peppery kick, and the zucchini makes it comforting, light, and yet creamy. My little guy loves it, too.

VEGETARIAN, PALEO, GF (VEGAN IF OMITTING THE CHEESE)

SERVES 2 AS A MAIN DINNER, OR 4 AS A SNACK OR STARTER

1 tablespoon olive oil

1 yellow onion, chopped fine

2 cloves garlic, minced

3 zucchini, diced

½ teaspoon salt

⅛ teaspoon white pepper

1 cup fresh basil leaves, roughly chopped

3 cups vegetable stock (for non-vegetarians chicken stock also works great)

2 cups arugula, chopped

Slivered almonds or grated Parmesan for garnish (optional)

Heat a pot on medium heat and add the olive oil. Add onion and garlic and sauté until translucent, about 3–5 minutes. Add zucchini, salt, pepper, and basil and sauté for 1 more minute.

Add the stock and cook for 5 minutes, or until the zucchini is tender. Turn the heat off; add in the arugula and stir.

To liquidize the soup, use a blender or immersion blender. Then pour all the soup back into the pot. Taste for salt and pepper and add more if needed.

Serve hot with a sprinkle of slivered almonds or grated Parmesan if desired.

raw green soup

On a hot summer day, I don't want to spend too much time in the kitchen, nor am I generally in the mood for a big, heavy meal. This soup is the perfect go-to for exactly those days—refreshing, cooling, and nourishing.

VEGAN, PALEO, GF SERVES 2 AS A LIGHT LUNCH OR STARTER

1 cucumber, halved

1 cup spinach, roughly chopped

¼ cup cilantro, roughly chopped

1 avocado, peeled, pitted, and halved

Juice of ½ lime

½ cup ice cold water

Sea salt to taste

¼ cup water

Dulse and chili flakes for garnish

Add all the ingredients, except the dulse and chili flakes, to a blender. Blend until smooth and creamy. Add a little more water if the soup seems too thick. Pour the soup into bowls and sprinkle with dulse and chili flakes.

✳ CUCUMBER BOOSTER

Cucumbers are really high in water and are therefore hydrating and cooling. It makes sense that they are at their freshest, ripest peak during the hottest days of summer. They are also a great source of the trace mineral silica, which is important for maintaining the strength of our connective tissue. This is what holds our whole body together (think muscles, tendons, and ligaments). The hydrating power combined with the high content of silica makes cucumbers a wonder food for maintaining dewy, fresh, and young-looking skin.

sweet pea soup

This is such a quick and easy meal to make, yet incredibly delicious and satisfying. It's a little sweet and a little spicy—with the cooling final touch to tie it all together. Frozen peas is one of those items that I always have in the freezer. In a pinch, when the fridge is looking dreadfully empty, this soup comes to the rescue.

VEGETARIAN, PALEO, GF SERVES 2

1 tablespoon butter

2 shallots, diced

2 cups frozen sweet peas

2 cups water

¼ teaspoon salt

⅛ teaspoon cayenne

15 mint leaves

1 dollop plain yogurt or coconut yogurt (nondairy alternative)

Chopped pistachios for garnish (optional)

In a medium-hot pot, melt the butter and add in the shallots. Sauté for 3 minutes until they are turning soft and translucent. Add in the frozen peas and sauté for 1 more minute. Add in the water, salt, and cayenne. Bring to a boil and then simmer for 5 minutes.

Add the mix to a blender, or turn the heat off and use an immersion blender in your pot. Add the mint leaves and blend until the soup is smooth and creamy.

Pour into two soup bowls. Add a dollop of yogurt on each and sprinkle with a few chopped pistachios.

coconut curry with bok choy and chicken

I love warm, comforting curries. The creamy sauce, the strong flavors, and the little spice kick are so satisfying. This is my version of a Thai green curry, a little bit milder than the ones I ate in Thailand, because I'm a wimp when it comes to spice. Feel free to add more heat if that's how you like it. I know my heat-loving husband would add some chili to this. Look for a curry paste that includes green chili, garlic, lemongrass, kaffir lime, ginger, and salt—and not much else.

PALEO, GF SERVES 4-6

1 tablespoon coconut oil

2 cloves garlic, chopped

1 tablespoon ginger, chopped fine

3 teaspoons green curry paste, or more if you like your food spicy

1 teaspoon ground coriander

½ cup fresh cilantro, chopped

1 tablespoon water

2 13.5 fl oz cans coconut milk (NOT light)

1½ pounds boneless, skinless chicken thighs or breasts, cut into 2-inch chunks

3 baby bok choys, cut in quarters the long way

1 cup sliced mushrooms

1 cup chopped baby spinach

1 tablespoon lime juice

1 tablespoon coconut sugar

1 tablespoon coconut aminos or gluten-free tamari

1 teaspoon sea salt

Cilantro for garnish

In a large saucepan or wok on medium heat, add the oil and garlic, ginger, curry paste, coriander, and fresh cilantro, along with a tablespoon of water. Cook for 1 minute, stirring continuously.

Add the coconut milk and bring to a simmer. Add the chicken and let it simmer for 5 minutes. Then add the bok choy and mushrooms (the pot might seem full, but the bok choy will wilt down). Simmer the soup for another 5 minutes.

Add in the spinach, lime juice, coconut sugar, and coconut aminos or tamari and stir. Simmer for 1 minute. Taste and add salt if needed.

Serve with cooked rice, quinoa, or green cauliflower rice.

raw green gazpacho

This is a fun green take on a Spanish classic. Traditionally, gazpacho is a cold soup with lots of tomatoes and basil. I kept the basil, garlic, and olive oil but swapped out the tomatoes for some flavorful and cooling greens. I hope you'll like it as much as I do.

VEGAN, PALEO, GF SERVES 2

½ cup chopped cucumber

1 clove garlic

1 spring onion, roughly chopped

½ cup green peas

½ cup chopped fennel

1 sprig fennel greens 1 cup chopped romaine

½ avocado

¼ cup chopped basil

1 cup water

¼ teaspoon salt or Herbamare

1 tablespoon olive oil

1 teaspoon apple cider vinegar

Chopped basil and sliced avocado for garnish

Add all the vegetables and basil, except the garnish, to a blender. Add in the water, salt, oil, and vinegar. Pulse the blender to chop the vegetables fine, without blending them too smoothly. You want some chunks and texture to this soup.

Cool the soup in the fridge for an extra refreshing touch or serve right away, with avocado and a little basil as garnish.

asparagus and spinach soup

This is a deliciously creamy, green, and fresh soup—especially delicious in the spring, when asparagus is in season and we crave some green goodness after a long winter.

PALEO, GF , VEGETARIAN (IF USING VEGETABLE STOCK)
SERVES 2 AS A MAIN DISH OR 4 AS A SNACK OR STARTER

1 tablespoon olive oil or ghee

1 leek, sliced (cleaned thoroughly, green parts removed)

2 cloves garlic

¼ teaspoon dried tarragon

1 sprig fresh thyme

Sea salt

1 quart chicken or vegetable stock

1 red-skinned potato, cubed (about 1½ cups)

¾ cups roughly chopped asparagus

4 big handfuls fresh spinach (about 5 cups)

Freshly ground pepper to taste

To a medium-hot pan add the oil or ghee. When it's hot, add in the leek and garlic, herbs, and a pinch of salt. Sauté for 3 minutes, stirring occasionally, until the leek has become soft and a bit translucent.

Add in the stock and potato and cook for 10–15 minutes, until the potato is tender. Add in the asparagus and cook for 2 minutes; then turn the heat off and stir in the spinach.

To make the soup creamy, once the spinach has wilted, either add the soup, in batches, to a blender or use an immersion blender right in the pot. Add the blended soup back to the pot, taste, and add more salt and freshly ground pepper if needed.

creamy spinach soup with egg boats

When I was growing up, spinach soup was a common occurrence at our house, and my mom often served it with a few egg boats floating in it. They looked pretty, were fun for us kids, and added more filling protein and good nutrients to our dinner. We would eat it with sliced rye bread and lots of butter!

VEGETARIAN, GF, PALEO SERVES 2

- 1 tablespoon olive oil, ghee, or butter
- 1 large onion, chopped
- 4 cloves garlic, minced
- 1 large red-skinned potato, cubed
- 1 cup vegetable stock
- ½ cup water
- 2 bay leaves
- 2 teaspoons sea salt or Herbamare
- ¼ teaspoon pepper
- 6 cups roughly chopped spinach
- Handful parsley, chopped
- 2 hard-boiled eggs

Heat the olive oil or butter, and sauté the onion and garlic. When the onion is translucent, add in the rest of the ingredients, except the spinach, parsley, and eggs, and let the mixture boil for about 15 minutes or until the potatoes are soft when poked with a fork.

Turn the heat off and add in the spinach and parsley (saving a little parsley for garnish). Let the soup steep for 2 minutes. Fish out the bay leaf and discard it. Add the soup to a blender or use an immersion blender to liquidize the mixture into a smooth, creamy soup.

Halve the hard-boiled eggs into four little "boats." Ladle the soup into two serving bowls and garnish each with two egg boats, a sprinkle of parsley, and some gluten-free croutons.

salads

Everyone can make a salad. And all countries, cultures, families, and individuals have their own go-to salads. As someone who's dabbled with healthy eating for a while, I've tried, tasted, made, and loved my fair share of salads. The possibilities are endless—from the simplest of green lettuce tossed with oil and lemon juice, to the most complex combinations. In this chapter you'll find a collection of some of my all-time favorite combinations. Some are simple, light, and perfect as a side or a light snack on hot days, while others contain more protein and maybe some roasted and cooked foods. There are arugula salads, kale salads, a different take on the classic Caesar salad, and even a few warm salads. Have fun!

shredded chicken and napa cabbage salad

This salad was inspired by my favorite Vietnamese salad. It is simple, without too many crazy ingredients, yet it tastes exotic and delicious. The secret is in the dressing . . . For the chicken, you could use leftovers from a rotisserie or roast chicken or some sliced, grilled chicken breast.

PALEO, GF SERVES 4

Dressing:

¼ cup fish sauce

1 tablespoon grated ginger

1 chili, seeds removed, thinly sliced (optional; adjust to your own spice preference)

1 clove garlic, grated

2 tablespoons lime juice

¼ cup water

2 teaspoons coconut sugar or syrup

Salad:

½ cup cut-up, cooked chicken

½ red or orange bell pepper

1 carrot

3 spring onions

1 head napa cabbage, washed well and sliced into strips

⅓ cup chopped cilantro leaves

⅓ cup roughly chopped cashews

1 tablespoon chia seeds

Mix all the dressing ingredients together in a bowl or jar and set aside.

With your fingers, shred the chicken into bite-size pieces. Drizzle the chicken with ¼ cup of the dressing and set it aside.

Cut up the bell pepper, carrot, and onions and add all the vegetables, the cilantro, and the cashews to a large mixing bowl. Pour the remaining dressing over and toss everything together well. Add the chicken and chia seeds. Give the salad another toss and serve.

warm beet greens, beet, and walnut salad

It's time to stop throwing away those beet greens and use the whole vegetable. I know beets are one of those vegetables many of you may both feel intimidated by (hello, pink fingers) and think you don't like (it's time to try some roasting). I hope this recipe will convert you all to beet lovers. Beets are chock-full of micronutrients, totally delicious, and naturally sweet. They help boost the body's detox function; they are loaded with antioxidants; and their natural sweetness can help satisfy a sweet tooth, so that dessert is less necessary.

VEGAN, PALEO, GF SERVES 4 AS A SIDE DISH

Olive oil

1 bunch of beets, with greens

Salt and pepper

⅓ cup chopped walnuts

1 tablespoon balsamic vinegar

Preheat the oven to 375°F and drizzle a baking sheet with some olive oil. Cut the greens off the beetroots, keeping a little stem on the beets. Wash and scrub the beets well. Cut the beets in four if they're on the smaller side or six if they are large.

Place the beets on the baking sheet and drizzle them with olive oil. Place in the oven and roast for 30 minutes.

Right before the 30 minutes are up, cook the beet greens: Wash them in a salad spinner and spin dry, chop the stems into chunks, and roughly tear up the leaves. Add 1 tablespoon olive oil to a pan and sauté the greens for a couple of minutes. Sprinkle with a little salt and freshly ground pepper.

To serve, place the greens on a plate and all the beets on top. Sprinkle with chopped walnuts and balsamic vinegar.

arugula, grapefruit, and goat cheese salad

Arugula is a leafy green that's full of flavor. It holds up well to other bold flavors but needs a little something refreshing to balance it out. Grapefruit and pecans work wonders in this combination, and the rich flavor of goat cheese goes well with arugula. You can use candied pecans here if you want to get fancy (and don't mind a little sugar). If you are not a fan of goat cheese, or prefer to avoid dairy, just leave out the cheese. The salad is delicious without it, too. Since you peel the grapefruit for the salad, you can probably squeeze enough grapefruit juice from the flesh left on the peel for the juice in the vinaigrette.

This salad is great for a light lunch or as a side or starter for your dinner party for two.

VEGETARIAN, GF SERVES 2

Shallot vinaigrette:

1 large shallot, chopped, about ½ cup

1 teaspoon Dijon mustard

1 teaspoon grapefruit juice

Juice and zest of ½ lemon

1 teaspoon apple cider vinegar

¼ cup olive oil

Salad:

6 cups arugula

⅓ cup roughly chopped pecans

½ cup crumbled goat or blue cheese

1 grapefruit, peeled and sliced

¼ red onion, thinly sliced

To make the vinaigrette, add all the ingredients except the oil to a blender. Turn the blender on low and mix all the ingredients. Then slowly start drizzling in the oil while the blender is going, so that it emulsifies.

Toss the arugula with the vinaigrette. Sprinkle in the nuts and cheese and add the onion and grapefruit. Toss again and serve.

arugula, lentil, goat cheese, and crispy apple salad

This is a filling yet light and crisp salad that I absolutely love. The lentils and goat cheese add a dose of protein, while the apples and currants provide some satisfying sweetness. The peppery arugula makes a perfect bed for it all.

The lentil part of this recipe is absolutely delicious on its own and holds in the fridge for days. It makes an easy, portable lunch option and even a great breakfast.

VEGETARIAN, GF SERVES 4

1 cup lentils

3 cups water

½ green apple, chopped

½ cup chopped walnuts

1 cup currants

½ cup chopped parsley

⅘ cups arugula

1 tablespoon olive oil

1 tablespoon apple cider vinegar

¼ cup crumbled goat cheese

Dressing:

1 tablespoon apple cider vinegar

1 teaspoon Dijon mustard

1 teaspoon raw honey

salt and pepper

1 tablespoon olive oil

Add lentils and water to a pot and bring to a boil. Turn the heat down and let simmer for 15–20 minutes. The lentils should be tender but still chewy. Set aside to cool.

In the meantime, prepare your dressing for the lentils. Combine all the ingredients for the dressing except the olive oil. Add the olive oil last, slowly drizzling it into the other ingredients, stirring continuously to create a creamy, smooth dressing that doesn't separate.

Once the lentils have cooled to room temperature, add in the apples, nuts, currants, and parsley and drizzle the dressing over. Mix well.

Add the arugula to a salad bowl and toss it with a tablespoon each of the oil and vinegar. Place the lentil mixture on top and sprinkle with goat cheese.

WALNUT BOOSTER

All nuts are an excellent source of healthy fats and fiber. But walnuts are a favorite of mine because they're one of the few nuts that contain omega-3 fatty acids, those anti-inflammatory, brain-boosting fats that most of us could eat a lot more of. They are also a great source of antioxidants, helping the body combat free-radical damage.

green slaw with soba noodles

I adore this colorful and vibrant dish. Food should look pretty and inviting, and including almost all the colors of the rainbow on a plate is pretty much as good as it gets. Here you have crispy fresh vegetables mixed with the ultimate comfort food— noodles. The fresh-tasting sauce is just almonds, lime, and ginger. No nasties here.

VEGAN, GF SERVES 4

1 packet 100% buckwheat soba noodles, or brown rice noodles (both are gluten free)

1 cup shaved or shredded brussels sprouts

1 large carrot, shredded

2 spring onions, chopped fine

1 cup seeded, peeled, and shredded cucumber

1 cup finely chopped kale

1 cup shredded purple cabbage

½ cup chopped cilantro

Dressing:

¼ cup almond butter

Juice and zest of 1 lime

½ tablespoon finely grated ginger

1 tablespoon coconut aminos or tamari

1 tablespoon tamarind paste (optional)

1 tablespoon maple syrup or coconut nectar

Garnish:

½ lime for garnish, quartered

A few sprigs of cilantro

Cook the noodles according to the package directions. Set aside to cool. Toss all the vegetables together in a large bowl.

In a small bowl, combine all the ingredients for the dressing and stir well until everything is combined. Pour half of the sauce over the vegetables and toss. Pour the other half over the noodles and toss.

Add the noodles to the vegetables. Combine and serve with a lime wedge and some cilantro as garnish.

✳ SERVING OPTION

You could also make this a warm dish. Just sauté all the vegetables with a little coconut oil. Toss the noodles in while they are still warm and pour the sauce over. Toss everything together, making sure the sauce gets distributed well. Serve with a sprinkle of cilantro as garnish.

dandelions with wild salmon

The bitter, pungent taste of dandelions holds up really well to fats and fatty foods like wild salmon. In this dish I've also added my favorite condiment, mustard, to add a little spice to it all. This is a perfect weeknight meal for two—quick to prepare, totally delicious, and healthy!

PALEO, GF SERVES 2

For the dandelion:

2 tablespoons olive oil

1 yellow onion, halved and sliced

2 cloves garlic, minced

1 bunch dandelion greens (about 4–6 cups), trimmed, washed (and still damp), and roughly chopped

Juice of ½ lemon

¼ teaspoon salt

Freshly ground pepper

For the salmon:

½ tablespoon olive oil

1 pound wild salmon, cut into two fillets

2 tablespoons Dijon mustard

¼ teaspoon salt

Freshly ground pepper

Preheat the oven to 375°F. Drizzle a little olive oil into an ovenproof dish and place the salmon on top. Smear each salmon fillet with 1 tablespoon of mustard and sprinkle with a little salt and pepper. Place the salmon in the oven for about 20–30 minutes, depending on the thickness of the fillets. Check your fish after 20 minutes and then add a little more cooking time if needed.

While the salmon is cooking, prepare your greens: Add 1 tablespoon olive oil to a medium-hot pan, add the onion and garlic and sauté for 3–5 minutes, until the onion is translucent. Add in the damp dandelion and allow the water from the leaves to help wilt the dandelion. Sauté for 2 minutes with the onion and garlic. Drizzle with the remaining olive oil, the lemon juice, salt, and pepper.

Serve the salmon fillets on top of a big bed of dandelion greens.

grilled caesar salad

When I first heard of this idea, I was intrigued and just had to try it. Luckily, I have a husband who loves a great fire, so at our next barbecue we tested this one out and—wow—it's a winner. Super simple and a perfect starter to a summer grill fest. (If you don't barbecue all that often, a grill pan would do just fine here.)

PALEO, GF SERVES 4

Dressing:

2 anchovies

2 garlic cloves, minced

2 tablespoons freshly squeezed lemon juice

2 teaspoons Dijon mustard

¼ teaspoon salt

¼ teaspoon coarsely ground black pepper

2 tablespoons apple cider vinegar

1 egg yolk

½ cup olive oil

Salad:

2 heads romaine lettuce

1 tablespoon olive oil

2 anchovies, chopped

¼ cup shaved Parmesan cheese (optional)

You can make your Caesar salad dressing either with a mortar and pestle or in a food processor. I chose the first option: Add the garlic and anchovies to the mortar and use the pestle to mash them together. Transfer to a bowl and add the lemon juice, mustard, salt, pepper, and vinegar and mix well with a whisk.

Add the egg yolk and whisk it in. Finally, drizzle the olive oil in slowly, whisking continuously, making a smooth dressing.

Chop the romaine lettuce heads in half lengthwise, and rub with some olive oil. Add the heads of romaine to your grill, with the cut side down. Leave on for a couple of minutes (depending on how hot your grill is) until the leaves start caramelizing and turning golden on the side that faces the grill.

Take the heads off and place on a plate with the cut side up. Drizzle with the dressing, letting it seep and drip down into the lettuce heads. Sprinkle with the chopped anchovies and, if you like, some shaved Parmesan. (You can absolutely leave out these two options, and the salad will still be yummy.)

✳ ANCHOVY BOOSTER

I love anchovies. Chances are you do, too—you just don't know it yet. They add a delicious, rich and salty flavor to dressings and sauces and go great on pizza, in pastas, and even on their own. Because these are whole fish fillets, they contain the fish's actual tiny bones, which are a great source of calcium. They are also a great source of potassium. Because they are such a small fish, the chances they contain mercury is really low compared larger fish such as swordfish and tuna.

summery
kale salad

I developed this recipe for the rooftop baby shower for my son. I knew it was going to be a big crowd on a hot day, so I went for something refreshing, healthy, and satisfying. I don't know about you, but I always get peckish at a party and hardly ever find a good-for-me option I can munch on. This is it.

VEGAN, PALEO, GF SERVES 2

1 bunch lacinato kale, stems removed, chopped into bite-size pieces

Juice of ½ lemon

1 tablespoon olive oil

Sprinkle of Himalayan sea salt

½ avocado

1 peach, pit removed, sliced

½ jicama, cut in small cubes

⅓ cup toasted hazelnuts

Add the kale to a bowl and pour the lemon juice, olive oil, and salt over it. Roll up your sleeves and massage the kale with your hands until it softens and gets bright and dark green. Add the avocado and massage that in, too.

Add the rest of the ingredients, finishing with a sprinkle of the jicama and hazelnuts.

✳ JICAMA BOOSTER

Jicama is sweet a potato relative. It has a bright white flesh and brown skin. Eaten raw, it's crispy and refreshing and perfect in slaws, salads, or just sliced. It also has a high water content, making it perfect for juicing. Nutritionally, it contains plenty of fiber and vitamin C yet is low in calories.

pumpkin and kale salad

I love the combination of roasted pumpkin, pumpkin seeds, and pumpkin seed oil. It's just such a fun way to really use the whole vegetable. Here they all come together on a bed of kale, one of the dark, leafy green vegetables that are easy to find in the winter and hearty enough to handle some roasted winter vegetable action. The stems are great for making green juice or vegetable stock.

VEGAN, PALEO, GF SERVES 2

- ½ small pumpkin (or about 2 cups uncooked pumpkin, butternut squash, or any other winter squash you'd like), cubed
- 1 teaspoon olive oil
- 1 bunch curly green or purple kale, washed, stems removed, and roughly chopped into bite-size pieces
- 1 tablespoon olive oil
- 1 tablespoon lemon juice
- ¼ teaspoon salt
- ½ cup pumpkin seeds
- 1 teaspoon pumpkin seed oil
- Freshly ground pepper
- ½ cup chopped parsley

Preheat the oven to 350°F. Place the pumpkin or winter squash on a baking sheet that's been greased with a little olive oil. Drizzle a little olive oil over the pumpkin and place in the oven for 20 minutes, or until the pumpkin cubes turn golden and soft.

Add the kale to a large mixing bowl and sprinkle with the olive oil, lemon juice, and salt. Massage the kale with your (very clean) hands until the leaves turn bright green and soften. Place the kale in a salad bowl.

Once the pumpkin is done, let it cool; then add it to the kale. Sprinkle the pumpkin seeds over and drizzle with the pumpkin seed oil, chopped parsley and some fresh ground pepper.

israeli salad

What makes this salad is super fresh ingredients and the chopping technique. Somehow chopping all the ingredients into tiny, half-inch cubes makes all the flavors blend into a delicious and refreshing salad. Fresh, seasonal heirloom tomatoes would be great in this salad. Try to use English or Persian cucumbers if you can find them, and use a good olive oil.

VEGAN, PALEO, GF SERVES 2

1 cucumber, seeds removed

2 large tomatoes, seeds removed

5 radishes

½ cup finely chopped parsley

1 tablespoon olive oil

Juice of ½ lemon

½ teaspoon sea salt, or to taste

Chop all the vegetables into equally sized, tiny cubes. Add to a salad bowl, add the parsley, and drizzle with olive oil, lemon juice, and salt. Toss well until all the ingredients are well mixed.

Serve with a dollop of hummus, sliced avocado, or olives.

✳ TOMATO BOOSTER

The tomato might just be one of the most commonly eaten vegetables (although technically a fruit) in the Western world today. It's rich in vitamin C and an antioxidant called lycopene. Lycopene has been shown to be specifically beneficial for fighting many kinds of cancer. And it turns out that the more you cook a tomato, the more lycopene you get, because the cooking process actually helps liberate the lycopene and make it more available to us.

warm winter salad with millet

This dish came to me in a lunchtime leftover frenzy. I happened to have the main ingredients for this salad in my fridge as leftovers, and when tossed together with a few fresh herbs and a dollop of hummus, they created a whole new delicious dish of their own.

VEGETARIAN, GF SERVES 2

½ cup millet

1 cup water

Pinch of sea salt

1 tablespoon olive oil

1 carrot

1 cup brussels sprouts

1 parsnip

1 small winter squash peeled and seeded

1 onion

½ cup chopped parsley

1 sprig thyme, chopped

1 sprig rosemary, chopped

Juice of ½ lemon

Ghee or grass-fed butter, melted

Sea salt and freshly ground pepper

Hummus or guacamole as garnish

Rinse the millet well and add it to a pot with the water and salt. Cover with the lid and bring to a boil; then turn the heat down and let it simmer for 30 minutes.

Once done, fluff it with a fork and set it aside.

Meanwhile, preheat the oven to 350°F. Chop the vegetables into similarly sized cubes and halve the brussels sprouts.

Drizzle olive oil into a baking dish, add the vegetables, and drizzle them with olive oil, too. Cover with tinfoil or a lid and bake for 10 minutes. Remove the tinfoil and bake for another 20 minutes, until the vegetables are tender and slightly golden.

Mix the roasted vegetables and millet in a bowl and stir in the chopped fresh herbs, the lemon juice, and melted butter. Add sea salt and freshly ground pepper to taste.

Add a big spoonful of hummus or guacamole on top. Serve immediately while still warm.

* WHAT IS MILLET?

Millet is quinoa's smaller and dryer sister – a tiny yellow seed packed with minerals, protein and fiber. It's naturally gluten free and high in protein. It was used in China as the main grain before rice became popular. It's still a widely used grain around the world due to its sturdiness and ability to grow in harsh conditions. It has soothing and warming properties, so it's great for cold and rainy days.

sardine salad

Fatty fish from cold water have the highest amounts of omega-3; choices include wild-caught salmon, sardines, herring, and small halibut. Smaller fish are less likely to contain dangerous levels of mercury. For an easy, always handy fish supply, buy canned fish. Sardines, anchovies, and wild salmon are good choices. Look for BPA-free cans.

PALEO, GF SERVES 2

1 teaspoon flax seed oil (optional)

1 tablespoon apple cider vinegar

¼ cup olive oil

Salt and pepper

1 bunch romaine lettuce, torn or cut into bite-size pieces

1 large roasted or boiled parsnip, chopped

¼ cup pumpkin seeds

1 can sardines (preferably in olive oil)

Combine the flax seed oil (if using) and the vinegar in the bottom of a salad bowl, whisking in the olive oil afterward to emulsify the dressing and avoid separation. Add salt and pepper to taste to complete the dressing.

Add the romaine on top and toss with the dressing. Sprinkle in the parsnip and pumpkin seeds and place the sardines on top.

❋ SARDINE BOOSTER

Sardines are small, fatty, cold-water fish loaded with omega-3 fatty acids. They have great anti-inflammatory benefits and help nourish the skin. They are also a good source of vitamin D and calcium, a great combination for promoting strong bones.

super-simple pea shoot salad with radishes

When you see pea shoots at the farmers market, grab them and make this simple salad as a refreshing springtime starter.

VEGAN, PALEO, GF SERVES 2 AS A SIDE DISH OR STARTER

2 cups pea shoots

4 radishes, thinly sliced (use a mandolin if you have one)

1 tablespoon extra virgin olive oil

1 tablespoon lemon juice

Sea salt

Freshly ground pepper

Wash and dry the pea shoots. Slice the radishes and toss with the pea shoots in a salad bowl. Drizzle with olive oil, lemon, salt, and pepper. Toss and serve.

❋ RADISH BOOSTER

Radishes are pungent, flavor-packed roots that come in many shapes and sizes and include the large, long, and white daikon, the Cherry Belle, and the Red Globe, among others. Radishes are full of trace minerals, including folic acid and potassium. They belong to the family of cruciferous vegetables and contain all of those great cancer-fighting benefits. Because radishes contain a few sulfur-based chemicals, they also help increase the flow of bile, which aids in the digestion of fat and supports a healthy gallbladder.

sides

A great side dish can elevate the simplest chicken, fish, or beans dinner to a delicious meal. Most of us tend to eat our greens this way—as a side dish to what ever 'main' dish we're making for dinner—anyway, so we might as well make them really tasty, as a way to keep weeknight dinners interesting. I hope this chapter will provide you with lots of inspiration and new ideas for what to do with those brussels sprouts or the big bunch of leafy greens that's staring at you from the crisper. And if you're trying to cut back on the starchy and refined carbohydrates (like potato chips, white rice, or white pasta), there are a few ideas on how to use vegetables instead.

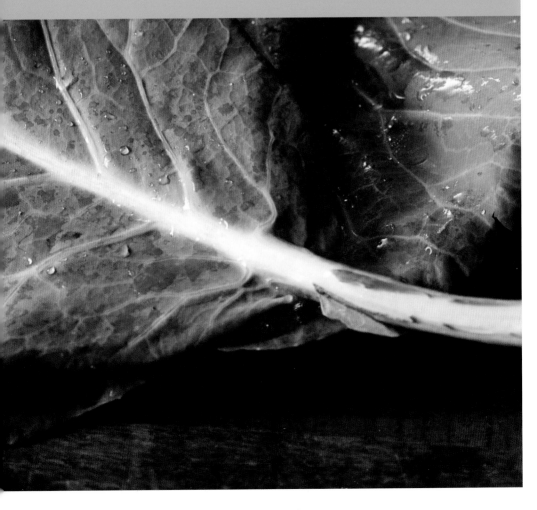

baked brussels sprouts with apple

This is a great side dish for any fall meal, but it's the ultimate side dish for a nice pork chop. The apples and apple cider add a tangy, refreshing touch, and baking the dish covered causes the juices to mix together and the brussels sprouts to become soft and tender.

VEGAN, PALEO, GF SERVES 4

3 cups trimmed and halved brussels sprouts

1 green, tart apple (such as Granny Smith, but any apple will do)

1½ tablespoons olive oil

2 tablespoons apple cider vinegar

Salt

Pepper

Preheat the oven to 375°F.

While the oven's heating, wash the apple and cut it into cubes, similar in size to the brussels sprout halves. Add the apples and sprouts to an ovenproof dish with a lid, such as a Dutch oven. Drizzle with olive oil, apple cider vinegar, and a bit of salt and pepper and toss to coat well. Put the lid on, and place the dish in the oven.

Stir after 15 minutes, then cook for another 15 minutes. When the time is up, remove the dish from the oven and let it cool slightly before serving.

Drizzle with olive oil, lemon, salt, and pepper. Toss and serve.

spicy and tangy roasted brussels sprouts

Bring on the heat! Brussels sprouts are hearty enough to handle bold and spicy combinations. Here I tossed them with some red pepper flakes and lemon zest for a bright and spicy side dish.

VEGAN, PALEO, GF SERVES 4

3 cups brussels sprouts, trimmed and halved

2 tablespoons olive oil

Juice and zest of a lemon

½ tablespoon red pepper flakes

Salt

Pepper

Preheat the oven to 375°F.

Add the brussels sprouts to a large mixing bowl. Drizzle with olive oil and lemon juice and sprinkle with lemon zest, red pepper flakes, and salt and pepper. Toss everything together using a large spoon (be careful not to get red pepper flakes on your hands—it can sting).

Transfer the sprouts mixture to a baking dish and place in the oven. Bake for 30 minutes, or until the brussels sprouts are turning golden and crispy. Serve hot.

honey mustard
brussels sprouts

Honey and Dijon mustard are a beloved and classic condiment combination for good reason—it works. It's a little sweet, sour, and spicy all at once. The sugar from the honey also helps caramelize the brussels sprouts, making them crispy on the outside and soft and gooey on the inside.

VEGETARIAN, PALEO, GF SERVES 4

3 cups trimmed and halved brussels sprouts

1 tablespoon raw honey

1 tablespoon Dijon mustard

2 tablespoons olive oil

Salt and pepper

Preheat the oven to 375°F. In a small bowl stir together the honey, mustard, and olive oil.

Pour the dressing over the brussels sprouts and toss until all the sprouts are covered well. Spread them on a baking sheet and sprinkle with salt and freshly ground pepper.

Place in the oven and bake for 30 minutes, tossing occasionally. The brussels sprouts are done when they're tender and the outside has turned golden and slightly crispy.

brussels sprouts salad with pear and bacon

I love salads. I love brussels sprouts and kale. And, yes, I too love bacon. This is one delicious combination of all those lovely things—deliciously sweet, smoky, and savory. These heartier greens stand up well to the fat and flavor of bacon, and the pear adds a nice sweetness to balance it all out. I could eat this every day. . .maybe even for breakfast.

PALEO, GF SERVES 4 (OR 2 AS A MAIN DISH)

1 cup bite-size pieces of bacon

2 shallots, finely chopped

4 cups total shredded brussels sprouts and chopped kale

1 pear, sliced

⅓ cup hazelnuts or walnuts, toasted and chopped

Dressing:

1 tablespoon Dijon mustard

1 tablespoon raw honey

1 tablespoon apple cider vinegar

1 tablespoon olive oil

Salt and pepper to taste

In a deep sauté pan, pot, or wok, fry the bacon. When it's turning golden, take it out but leave the fat.

Add the shallots to the pot and sauté for 1 minute, then add the shredded vegetables. Sauté for 2–3 minutes. Add the pear and sauté for 1 more minute.

Take off the heat and add the bacon and nuts. Pour the dressing over and toss well to coat the whole salad. Serve warm.

sautéed kale

Sautéed kale is super quick to make, adds lots of nutrients and offers endless possibilities. This recipe works for all the dark, leafy greens, such as Swiss chard, broccoli rabe, and all the different kales.

VEGAN, PALEO, GF SERVES 4

1 bunch kale

¼ cup water

Sea salt

1 tablespoon olive oil

Wash your kale and dry well using a salad spinner.

Add the water to a sauté pan (a slightly deeper frying pan) and bring it to a boil. Turn the heat down to medium.

Add the kale to the simmering water and let it steam. When there's only a little water left, add the salt and olive oil. Toss all the ingredients together and sauté for 1 more minute.

FLAVOR OPTIONS

For different flavors, try adding these combinations when there's only a little water left in the pan, instead of the salt and olive oil:

Ginger/Lime
1 tablespoon grated ginger
Juice and zest of ½ lime
Garlic/Hot Pepper
cloves garlic, chopped fine
½ teaspoon red pepper flakes, or more if you like it hot
Coconut/Cashew
Switch out the olive oil in the basic recipe with 1 tablespoon coconut oil.
2 tablespoons shredded coconut or coconut flakes
¼ cup chopped cashews
Umami
1 tablespoon coconut aminos
1 tablespoon dulse flakes
Sweet Mustard
1 tablespoon spicy Dijon mustard
1 tablespoon raw honey

collard greens with leek and almonds

Collard greens get melt-in-your-mouth soft when you cook them, and the crunchy almonds and sweet leeks elevate the dish to restaurant levels.

To cut collard greens, first remove the thickest part of the stem. Stack the leaves on top of each other and fold the long side over once. Cut into 1-inch strips. Unfold and wash well. Use a salad spinner if you have one.

VEGETARIAN, VEGAN (IF USING COCONUT OIL) PALEO, GF SERVES 4

1 tablespoon butter (ghee or coconut oil would work great, too)

2 cloves garlic

1 leek, green parts removed, washed well, and cut into ½-inch pieces

1 bunch collard greens, cut into strips

Salt and pepper

¼ cup roughly chopped almonds

Add the butter to a medium-hot skillet and let it melt. Add the garlic and sauté for 2 minutes; then add the leeks and sauté for another 3 minutes, until the leeks are soft and translucent.

Add the collard green strips little by little and let them wilt down. Once all the collard greens are soft and bright green, they're done.

Season with salt and pepper and sprinkle with chopped almonds and serve.

✳ HOW TO CLEAN LEEKS

There's often a bit of dirt and sand caught inside the layers of a leek, so thorough washing is required. I prefer to cut the leek first and then wash it. First, remove the top green part (and save it for making vegetable stock), then cut along the leek lengthwise before slicing the whole leek into ½-inch disks. Add the chopped leek to a strainer or salad spinner and soak it in water, swooshing it around to remove any sand and dirt. Drain, rinse again, and spin or shake dry.

steamed collard greens with almond sauce

This dish was another one of those happy accidents when I had to get dinner on the table using only what was on hand. This side dish turned out so good that when I first threw this sauce together, I licked the bowl. . . .I used a raw, creamy almond butter, but most versions should work.

VEGAN, PALEO, GF SERVES 4

1½ tablespoons almond butter

1 teaspoon finely ground ginger

1 teaspoon coconut aminos (or tamari)

½ teaspoon turmeric

½ teaspoon sea salt

2-4 teaspoons water

1 bunch collard greens, thickest part of the stems trimmed off, washed well

Add all the ingredients except the water and collard greens to a bowl and mix well. Slowly add the water, 1 teaspoon at a time, until you have a drizzle-able sauce. Set aside.

Add about an inch of water to a pot and place your steam basket in the pot. Bring the water to a boil. Place the collard greens in the basket and steam for about 1 minute, or until the leaves soften and turn bright green. Remove the greens and let any excess water drain off.

Place on a serving platter and drizzle with the almond sauce.

steamed vegetables with tahini

Tahini is just blended up sesame seeds and is easy to turn into a dip or sauce with just a few other ingredients. If you're really hungry, serve this dish alongside some brown rice and adzuki beans, and you'll have a perfectly balanced macrobiotic plate.

VEGAN, PALEO, GF SERVES 2

Veggies:

½ winter squash (butternut, acorn, or other), cut into 2-inch cubes

1 cup sliced turnip, cut into 2-inch cubes

½ daikon radish, halved and cut into 2-inch cubes

1 zucchini, cut into 2-inch cubes

A few broccoli or broccolini florets

Tahini sauce:

2 tablespoons tahini

½ lemon

4 tablespoons water

¼ teaspoon salt

Add an inch of water to a pot and place your steam basket in the pot. Add the lid and bring the water to boil.

Place your vegetables in the basket, with the hardest ones (the ones that require the most cooking) at the bottom and broccoli or broccolini on top. Steam with the lid on for 2–3 minutes.

In the meantime, stir your tahini sauce ingredients together in a bowl, adding the water little by little while stirring, until you reach the desired thick but liquid consistency.

Place the vegetables in a bowl or on a plate and drizzle with the tahini sauce (or simply use it as a dipping sauce).

swiss chard with lemon and ginger

I love this tangy and colorful side dish. It's delicious on top of some grains, alongside fish, or even as a burger topping. Lemon and ginger help boost digestion, and the fiber in the greens is good for your belly.

VEGAN, PALEO, GF SERVES 4

1 tablespoon olive oil

1 red onion, chopped

1 tablespoon finely chopped ginger

1 bunch rainbow chard, trimmed, washed, and chopped into 1-inch strips

Juice and zest of ½ lemon

1 tablespoon coconut aminos or gluten-free tamari

Salt

Add the oil to a medium-hot pan and sauté the onion for 3 minutes, or until it's soft and translucent.

Add in the chopped collard stems and ginger and sauté for another minute. Then add the chard. Let the chard wilt down before adding the lemon and coconut aminos. Do a taste test and add a little salt if needed.

Toss together and serve hot.

✳ GINGER BOOSTER

Ginger is one of the most powerful anti-inflammatory agents in the plant world. It is used to relieve the symptoms of arthritis and osteoporosis and has also been shown to decrease muscle pain and soothe stomach aches, nausea, and flatulence. A fun fact you may enjoy is that ginger has been celebrated as an aphrodisiac for centuries.

steamed cabbage with dulse butter

This is such a simple dish, and it brings me right back to my childhood in Norway. Fresh cabbage, lightly steamed, with a big dollop of butter was a staple on our spring dinner table. This is a great side dish for any fish or on top of cooked grains such as buckwheat or quinoa.

VEGETARIAN, GF SERVES 4

1 head cabbage

4 tablespoons grass-fed butter

1 tablespoon dulse flakes

Ahead of time: Take the butter out of the fridge far enough ahead that it has time to get really soft. Then add it to a small bowl with the dulse. Stir until well combined.

When you're ready to prepare the recipe, cut the cabbage into eight equally sized wedges. In a pot, bring 1 ½ cup of water to a boil and add a steam basket. Add the cabbage, put the lid on, and steam for about 5 minutes, until the cabbage is fork tender.

To serve, place two pieces of steaming hot cabbage on each plate and add 1 tablespoon of butter on top. Let it melt down over the cabbage . . .

✳ DULSE BOOSTER

Dulse is a seaweed with reddish color and a salty flavor. You can find it in large pieces or in small flakes that are perfect for sprinkling on salads and grains. Like all seaweed, it's a great source of minerals, especially iodine—an important precursor to making thyroid hormones. Thyroid hormones stimulate energy production, influence metabolism, and support growth of hair and nails.

green cauliflower "rice"

Many of us are trying to find ways to eat more nutrient-dense vegetables and fewer starchy foods that are high in carbohydrates. It's a great tool for weight loss, but also for anyone trying to improve digestion—or just improving energy overall. This is no dish of compromise. It's a delicious, comforting, and light take on rice, with a chewy texture and fresh flavor. Try it. Your life may change forever.

VEGAN, PALEO, GF SERVES 4

1 head cauliflower, cut into large florets

1 tablespoon coconut oil

2 shallots, chopped fine

1 cup chopped spinach

¼ teaspoon salt

½ cup chopped cilantro

Juice of ½ lime

To turn the cauliflower into rice, use one of the following three methods:

In a food processor: Add the cauliflower to the food processor. Be careful not to pack the food processor too fully; do it in a couple of batches. Turn the machine on and process until the cauliflower is chopped into what resembles rice.

In a Vitamix dry: Add a handful of cauliflower florets to the blender. Turn it on to level 2 and use the tamper to push the cauliflower down toward the blades. Once all the cauliflower is finely chopped into what resembles rice, empty the container into a bowl and go again. Repeat until all the cauliflower is chopped.

In a Vitamix wet: You can also chop the cauliflower by adding water to the blender until the florets float and then turning it on to level 2. I found that my cauliflower got chopped a bit too fine when I used this method, but it still tasted delicious, and this is a super-quick way to do it.

Add the coconut oil to a sauté pan over medium heat. Add the shallots and sauté for 3 minutes, until translucent. Add the cauliflower and spinach, sprinkle with salt, and sauté for another 5 minutes. Remove from the heat and add the cilantro and lime juice.

Serve hot alongside your favorite fish or topped with any beans or lentils you like and avocado.

✳ CAULIFLOWER BOOSTER

Cauliflower is another member of the cruciferous vegetable family, and, like its siblings, it is rich in cancer-preventing compounds. Its taste and texture also make it a fantastic substitute for more starch-loaded white foods such as rice and potato. Raw cauliflower is a great source of vitamin K and C.

cauliflower tabbouleh

This crispy, crunchy side dish is another take on the traditional Middle Eastern grain dish. It's refreshingly lemony and minty and works great on its own, as part of a hummus platter, or as a side dish for fish, chicken, or lamb.

VEGAN, PALEO, GF SERVES 4

1 head cauliflower

1 cup chopped tomatoes (about 2 medium tomatoes)

1 cup chopped English or Persian cucumber

1 cup chopped green bell pepper

2 spring onions, chopped

1½ cups chopped curly kale

½ cup finely chopped parsley

½ cup finely chopped mint

Juice of ½ lemon

3 tablespoons olive oil

¼ teaspoon salt

Freshly ground pepper

Finely chop the cauliflower into small, grain-like pieces. You can follow one of the methods given in the recipe for Green Cauliflower "Rice" on page 126, or just use a knife.

Add all the chopped vegetables and herbs to a bowl and mix well. Drizzle in the lemon juice, olive oil, salt, and pepper. Mix it all well and do a taste test. Add more lemon juice, salt, or pepper if needed.

sautéed fiddleheads

Fiddleheads are a super seasonal (as in only available for a short time of year, in season) wild spring vegetable. They are bright green and spiral shaped and remind me of a little snail house. Because they are so fresh and available for such a short time, I keep it very simple when preparing them. Make sure to get them from a reputable source, and cook them completely.

VEGAN, PALEO, GF SERVES 4

5 cups water

2 cups fiddleheads, washed and trimmed

2 tablespoons olive oil

3 cloves garlic, chopped fine

Salt and pepper

In a medium-size pot, bring 5 cups of water to boil and add your fiddleheads. Let them boil for about 10 minutes, until they are fork tender. Drain and set aside.

In a skillet, add the olive oil and once hot, add the garlic. Let the garlic infuse the oil for about 2 minutes and then add the fiddleheads. Toss everything together and sauté for another 2 minutes. Sprinkle with salt and freshly ground pepper to taste.

broccolini, cherry tomato, and kale skillet

This is a delicious, Italian-influenced, one-pot dish. It contains lots of antioxidants yet is made with easily available, simple ingredients. It's perfect just as it is, or as a side dish alongside a grass-fed steak, or even tossed with pasta.

4–5 broccolini

2 tablespoons olive oil

3 cloves garlic

½ red onion, sliced

4 cups chopped lacinato kale

1 cup halved cherry tomatoes

1 cup halved and sliced zucchini

Sea salt and freshly ground black pepper

Bring a pot of water to a boil and add a steam basket. Place the broccolini in the basket and steam for 2–3 minutes. Remove the broccolini from the heat and set aside.

Add the olive oil to a medium-hot skillet and stir in the garlic, continuing to stir as the garlic flavors the oil. Take care not to burn the garlic. Add in the red onion and sauté for 3 minutes; then add the kale. Sauté for 1 more minute, or until the kale has wilted. Add the cherry tomatoes, zucchini, and steamed broccolini.

Sprinkle sea salt and grind fresh pepper over the whole dish and serve in the skillet for a rustic and wholesome side dish.

roasted broccoli with parmesan

This is an all-grown-up, upscale version of a children's favorite. Parmesan is a great cheese for cooking, since even a small amount adds a lot of salty, delicious flavor. Look for real, raw Parmesan if possible.

VEGETARIAN, GF SERVES 6

2–3 heads broccoli, cut into small florets

¼ cup olive oil

2 teaspoons salt

Generous amount of freshly ground pepper

1 cup grated Parmesan or Parmigiano Reggiano

Preheat the oven to 400°F.

Place the broccoli florets on a baking sheet lined with parchment paper and drizzle them with oil. Sprinkle with salt and pepper and the grated Parmesan. Use your fingers to mix everything together evenly.

Bake for 11–15 minutes, or until the broccoli is slightly crisp and golden, and the cheese has melted.

snacks & sauces

Who says that newfound greens obsession I hope you have needs to end with salads and sides? Add more nutrient-dense greens to your snacks, too, and reap the benefits of having more energy, fewer cravings, glowing skin, and a better mood. In this chapter you'll find multiple ideas for how to make your own kale chips in any flavor combination you may fancy, plus dip options for your party platter of crudités and crackers.

Kale Chips Five Ways

These chips are a great, healthy treat when you're longing for a bit of salty crunch. They are the perfect replacement for potato chips and are a true crowd pleaser. They are also a great portable snack. Use a mason jar or other solid container so that the chips don't get completely crushed in transit. Making them for a big crowd? Simply double or triple the recipe.

The recipes that follow are for a few varieties that I love, but don't let that stop you. Get inspired by your favorite chip flavors or simply what you have in your pantry and have fun with it.

coconutty kale chips

Coconuts are loaded with weight-loss-boosting benefits and satisfying healthy fats. These kale chips are a fabulous snack when you're a little hungry and something sweet-tasting just seems inevitable.

VEGAN, PALEO, GF SERVES 4

1 bunch kale, stems removed, torn into bite-size pieces

1 tablespoon coconut oil

1 tablespoon coconut nectar (honey or maple syrup works great, too)

2 tablespoons shredded coconut

Preheat the oven to 375°F and line a baking sheet with parchment paper.

Toss all the ingredients together in a bowl, making sure all the kale leaves are covered in oil and the coconut is evenly distributed. Spread the kale out on the lined baking sheet.

Bake for 15–20 minutes. Make sure to open the oven and toss the leaves around a few times, rearranging them into a single layer each time to make sure they get nice and crispy. Let them cool before serving.

vegan cheesy kale chips

Sometimes your cravings for something cheesy just take over. That's when it's good to have this little sucker up your sleeve.

VEGAN, PALEO, GF SERVES 4

1 bunch kale, stems removed, torn into bite-size pieces

1 tablespoon olive oil

½ teaspoon sea salt, preferably freshly ground Himalayan sea salt

2–3 tablespoons vegan Parmesan such as Parma (or 1 tablespoon nutritional yeast)

Preheat the oven to 350°F and line a baking sheet with parchment paper.

Toss all the ingredients together in a bowl, making sure all the kale leaves are covered in oil and "cheese." Spread the kale out on the lined baking sheet.

Bake for 15–20 minutes. Make sure to open the oven and toss the leaves around a few times, rearranging them into a single layer each time to make sure they get nice and crispy. Let them cool before serving.

whole-leaf kale chips

This is the prettiest presentation of them all and an impressive party trick. The whole kale leaf crinkles up and becomes crisp and easy to hold. It's the perfect finger snack.

VEGAN, PALEO, GF SERVES 2

10 leaves lacinato kale

1–2 tablespoons olive oil

1 teaspoon sea salt

Preheat the oven to 375°F. Wash the kale leaves and pat them dry with a towel. Lay them out on a baking sheet and drizzle with olive oil and salt, making sure every leaf gets a little touch.

Bake in the oven for 5 minutes or until the edges are starting to brown and the leaves feel dry and crispy. Watch out—they go from under done to burnt very quickly.

Serve! These are really pretty served in a large bowl in the middle of the table. . . if they make it that far.

salt & vinegar kale chips

This is an inspired take on a classic potato chip favorite, but without all the additives, sodium, and seed oil. You're welcome.

VEGAN, PALEO, GF SERVES 4

1 bunch kale, stems removed, torn into bite-size pieces

1 tablespoon olive oil

1½ tablespoons apple cider vinegar

½ teaspoon sea salt

Preheat the oven to 350°F and line a baking sheet with parchment paper.

Add the torn kale leaves to a bowl and drizzle with olive oil, vinegar, and salt. Toss and mix well until every leaf is coated. Spread the leaves out on a baking sheet. Make sure not to overlap them. Give the leaves plenty of room—that way they'll get crisp and not soft and soggy.

Bake for 15–20 minutes. Make sure to open the oven and toss the leaves around a few times, rearranging them into a single layer each time to make sure they get nice and crispy. Let them cool before serving.

lime and chili
kale chips

This is my twist on a classic South American flavor combination that never fails: chili and lime. A little tangy, with a serious kick, these chips are sure to get your taste buds excited.

VEGAN, PALEO, GF SERVES 2

1 bunch kale, stems removed, torn into bite-size pieces

1 tablespoon olive oil

Juice and zest of 1 lime

2 teaspoons chili powder (or cayenne pepper)

Preheat the oven to 350°F and line a baking sheet with parchment paper.

Toss all the ingredients together in a bowl, making sure all the kale leaves are covered in oil, lime, and chili powder.

Bake for 15–20 minutes. Make sure to open the oven and toss the leaves around a few times, rearranging them into a single layer each time to make sure they get nice and crispy. Let them cool before serving.

brussels sprout chips

This recipe happened upon me as a happy accident. Every time I roast brussels sprouts, a few of the outer leaves fall off the bulb and end up being cooked into perfectly crisp chips. Picking them right off the baking sheet might just be one of my favorite treats. So, I figured, why not make a whole tray of brussels sprout leaves? Mmm.

VEGAN, PALEO, GF SERVES 2 (OR JUST YOU IF YOU LOVE THESE AS MUCH AS I DO)

6–10 brussels sprouts

1 tablespoon olive or coconut oil

¼ teaspoon sea salt

Preheat the oven to 350°F and line a baking sheet with parchment paper. Wash and trim the bottom off the brussels sprouts. Peel the outer leaves off—they should come off pretty easily. Keep going, peeling off leaves, until you're left with a small bunch of leaves that seem difficult to peel off. Save these for another dish or roast on their own.

Add the leaves to a mixing bowl and drizzle with oil and salt. Toss well until all the leaves are coated. Spread the leaves out on a baking sheet. Make sure not to overlap them. Give them plenty of room, so they'll get crisp.

Bake for 15–20 minutes, checking every few minutes for leaves that are crisp and starting to brown. Remove those and keep on baking the rest until all are done.

Serve as a snack or a side dish with dinner. Yum!

cheesy vegan spinach dip

Party dips can be dangerous things. You never know exactly what's in them, yet you know they can't be good for you. So I came up with my own spin on a favorite—the cheesy spinach dip.

VEGAN, PALEO, GF MAKES ENOUGH TO PLEASE A PARTY CROWD (ABOUT 2 CUPS)

1 cup cashews, soaked 1–3 hours in pure water

1 cup water

2 cloves garlic

2 cups baby spinach, gently pressed down in the measuring cup to measure

2 tablespoons nutritional yeast

½ teaspoon salt

1 scallion, chopped fine

Drain and rinse the nuts. Then add them to a blender or food processor with a cup of water, garlic, spinach, nutritional yeast, and salt.

Blend until the mixture is smooth and then gently stir in the scallion, saving a few pieces for garnish. Pour or spoon into a serving bowl. Serve with organic corn chips, crackers, or crudité.

Bake for 15–20 minutes. Make sure to open the oven and toss the leaves around a few times, rearranging them into a single layer each time to make sure they get nice and crispy. Let them cool before serving.

✳ NUTRITIONAL YEAST BOOSTER

These yellow flakes taste a bit like cheese but contain no dairy and are a go-to for vegans with cheese cravings. But they are a source of more than cheesy flavor. They're rich in B-complex vitamins and are a complete protein. Vitamin Bs are skin-strengthening and help convert food into energy. So even if you enjoy real cheese from time to time, there's value in nutritional yeast for you.

green hummus

Why not make an all-time favorite healthy snack even healthier by adding some greens and herbs? Making your own hummus is a lot easier than you would think, and the taste is superior to the stuff you buy premade. The best part is that you get to control how much and what kind of oil you use.

VEGAN, GF MAKES ENOUGH TO PLEASE A PROPER PARTY CROWD (ABOUT 2 CUPS)

3½ cups canned garbanzo beans (about two 15-ounce cans)

2 cups spinach, loosely packed

1 cup arugula, loosely packed

¼ cup cilantro

¼ cup diced green onion

1 clove garlic

Juice of ½ lemon

Sea salt and fresh cracked black pepper to taste

1 cup olive oil

Splash of water if needed

Drain and rinse the canned beans well. Add all the ingredients, except the oil and water, to a blender or food processor and turn it on low, combining everything while slowly drizzling in the olive oil.

Check the consistency and taste for enough salt and pepper. Add a little water and salt if needed. Blend again and serve with your favorite raw vegetables or crackers or use in wraps and sandwiches.

dandelion pesto

Dandelion is a peppery, spicy, and bitter wild green that is a powerful detox booster and loaded with minerals. This pesto is amazing tossed with some fresh zucchini noodles or pasta or poured over steamed or roasted vegetables. It would also be great stirred in to any cooked grains or on boiled potatoes. The bold flavor stands up to meat really well, too, so you could try it at your next barbecue.

VEGAN, PALEO, GF MAKES ABOUT 1½ CUPS

2 cups dandelion greens, roughly chopped

¾ cup olive oil

3–4 cloves garlic

1 teaspoon fine sea salt

2 tablespoons vegan Parmesan (made from nuts, salt, and nutritional yeast) or grated Parmesan cheese

½ cup pine nuts

Toast the pine nuts by adding them to a dry pan and placing it over low heat on top of the stove. Keep moving the nuts around until they turn light golden and you can smell a wonderful nutty aroma.

Add all the ingredients to a blender or food processor. Pulse until everything is chopped and well combined. You can keep going until you have a smooth sauce or stop while it's a bit chunky. However you like it. I go for a smooth pesto myself . . .

✳ PINE NUT (PIGNOLI) BOOSTER

This creamy, rich, and delicious nut is the classic pesto nut. It contains more protein than any other nut and is a great source of healthy fats, minerals, and some B vitamins. The nutrient combo in these little powerhouses are the perfect packet for combating heart disease, and, thankfully, they are darned delicious, too.

AVOCADO
BOOSTER

Avocados are 20 percent fats and the richest fruit source of fats there is. They're a much better source of potassium than bananas and their high amount of oleic acid can help support healthy cholesterol levels. Avocados are loaded with vitamin E, which is a well-known skin nutrient that helps protect our skin cells from environmental damage.

creamy
avocado dip,
sauce, or dressing

This is a perfect and easy one-stop sauce—delicious, full of healthy fats, and very versatile. It's great as a salad dressing, perfect as a dip for crudité or seed crackers, and delicious with fish. I love it poured over grains or steamed vegetables. In fact, it would be perfect on the Bowl Full of Goodness on page 186.

VEGAN, PALEO, GF SERVES 6

2 avocados

1 cup baby spinach

¼ cup cilantro

2 cloves garlic

Juice of 1 lemon (or lime)

2 tablespoons apple cider vinegar

2 tablespoons olive oil

¼ teaspoon salt

Pinch of pepper

2–4 tablespoons water (as needed for the desired consistency of the sauce)

Add all the ingredients, except the water, to a blender; even an immersion blender should do here. Blend well, starting on a slow speed.

Add in the water little by little until you have the thickness you desire. Taste and add salt and pepper as needed.

Serve with crudité vegetables or your chips of choice. Try it with some fish or chicken or as a salad dressing. It works great massaged into raw kale or thinned a little and poured over tomatoes.

mains

There are lots of easy ways to incorporate greens into your more typical mains and dinner dishes, too. In this chapter you'll find favorites such as fried rice, pasta and egg dishes, all with a healthy twist. As much as I love cooking, I also love to eat out, explore new dishes, and get inspired by different cuisines. So look for a little bit of Italian, a little Vietnamese, a little Thai, and a touch of farm-to-table in this chapter. Because that's how I like to eat. I hope you'll like it, too.

green lasagna

When I was a kid, lasagna was one of my definite favorite dishes. It's real comfort food and to this day reminds me of dinners with my family. On a recent trip to visit them all, I came up with this version in my mom's kitchen. It's a vegan version that is a lot lighter than the traditional lasagna—without the béchamel sauce and white pasta and loaded with greens and fresh vegetables instead.

VEGAN, PALEO, GF SERVES 4–6

Sauce:

2 15-ounce cans butter beans (3 cups)

Juice of ½ lemon

¼ teaspoon salt

½ cup water

2 cloves garlic

½ cup olive oil

Spinach layer:

1 tablespoon olive oil

3 cloves garlic

2 bags baby spinach

Salt and pepper

Remaining layers:

6–8 tomatoes, sliced and seeds removed

1½ zucchini, sliced thinly lengthwise to resemble pasta

5 artichoke hearts, cut into six wedges

½ cup basil, chopped

Preheat the oven to 350°F.

To make the sauce, add all the sauce ingredients to a blender, except the olive oil. Start the blender and once the ingredients are combined, start drizzling in the oil slowly. Add a little more water if the sauce seems too thick. Set aside.

To make the spinach layer, heat the olive oil over medium heat and add the garlic. Sauté for 2 minutes; then add the spinach little by little, letting it wilt down before adding more. Sprinkle in salt and pepper. Once all the spinach is sautéed, turn the heat off and set the pan aside.

To prepare the remaining layers, layer your vegetables and sauce in a deep baking dish (a 9-inch pan works well). Start with tomatoes, sprinkle basil over and add a layer of sliced zucchini. Add a layer of sauce, layer on tomatoes and basil and add all the cooked spinach as a thick layer. Lay zucchini on top and add a layer of sauce. Place the artichoke wedges down as a layer and lay tomatoes on top. End by sprinkling some basil over the whole dish.

Place in the oven and bake for 20 minutes. Take it out and let it cool for 10 minutes (the tomatoes get piping hot).

Serve with a green salad. A glass of red wine is optional.

fried rice with greens

VEGETARIAN, GF SERVES 2

1 cup wild rice, uncooked

1 tablespoon coconut oil

1 onion, diced

2 cloves garlic, minced

1 tablespoon chopped ginger

2 cups chopped broccoli rabe or broccolini

¼ cup sweet green peas

1 teaspoon fish sauce

1 teaspoon coconut aminos

Juice and zest of ½ lime

2 eggs

Cook the wild rice in 2½ cups water for about 45 minutes, or until the water has evaporated and the rice is tender.

Add the coconut oil to a medium-hot pan and then add in the onion, garlic, and ginger. Sauté for 3 minutes, or until the onion is soft and translucent. Add in the broccolini (or broccoli rabe) and peas and sauté for another 2 minutes.

Add in the cooked rice, mix well, and drizzle in the fish sauce and coconut aminos. Let it all cook for 1 more minute; then pour the fried rice mix into serving bowls and sprinkle with the lime juice and zest.

Add a little more coconut oil to the pan if needed and fry the eggs, keeping the yolk whole and without flipping the eggs. Once the eggs are cooked, add one on top of each bowl of fried rice and serve immediately. Before actually tucking in to the dish, use a chopstick or fork to poke the egg yolk and gently mix the egg into the dish.

spring risotto with asparagus and spring greens

Creamy risotto is such a lovely meal—and it is truly a labor of love. It takes time and requires your full attention, to continually ladle in the warm stock and stir the risotto till it becomes creamy perfection. And is then devoured, with lots of compliments to the chef.

This is a clean, allergy-friendly and healthy version of risotto without cheese. However, if you love cheese and want to go all out, add in a cup of grated Parmesan.

GF, VEGAN (IF USING VEGETABLE STOCK) SERVES 4

1 quart chicken or vegetable stock (I use homemade chicken broth)

1 tablespoon olive oil

2 tablespoons garlic scapes or cloves, minced

1½ cups grated daikon radish

1 teaspoon Italian herb seasoning (with dried basil and thyme, or just add those herbs by themselves)

¼ teaspoon salt

1 cup Arborio rice

Juice and zest of 1 lemon

1 cup broccoli florets

1 cup sweet peas (fresh or frozen)

1 cup trimmed and chopped asparagus

1 cup chopped zucchini

2 cups spinach or arugula

2 tablespoons chopped basil

Freshly ground black pepper

¼ cup toasted pine nuts for garnish

Heat the stock in a pot on the stove. Once it simmers, turn the heat down to low. Measure, chop and prepare all your ingredients. Once you start cooking the rice, you don't want to leave the risotto pot.

Pour the olive oil into a medium-hot pan and add the garlic, stirring often. Let it simmer for 1 minute. Add the grated daikon radish, Italian seasoning, and salt. Sauté for 2 minutes.

Add the rice and lemon juice and ladle in your first spoonful of stock. Stir continuously. Once the stock is absorbed, add in another spoonful and continue stirring. Keep going this way until all the stock is used up—in about 15–20 minutes.

Add in the peas, asparagus, and zucchini and stir for another 2 minutes.

Finally, add the lemon zest, spinach, and basil and combine everything.

Taste the risotto and add more salt and pepper as needed. Serve with a sprinkle of toasted pine nuts on top.

To toast pine nuts:

To a dry pan on medium heat, add the pine nuts. Gently toss them around until they turn golden and fragrant. Remove from the heat and set aside.

✳ ASPARAGUS BOOSTER

Asparagus is a low-calorie vegetable with lots of fiber, minerals, antioxidants, and even protein. It's maybe best known for its diuretic benefits; it helps to reduce water retention and bloating.

raw collard greens wraps with tamarind sauce

Collard greens are the perfect wrap alternative. The leaves are nice and big and sturdy enough to handle some rolling, pulling, and stuffing. This wrap is a raw version in which I've combined some deliciously simple and tropical ingredients with a wonderful, tangy dipping sauce. Serve it as lunch, a party pleaser, or a dinner teaser . . .

Collard greens can be used as a wrapper for almost anything. Try stuffing them with hummus and avocado, curried chicken salad, or smoked salmon. Or try a new twist on any of your favorite sandwich ingredients: roasted vegetables and goat cheese, BLT, tomato and mozzarella, or roasted turkey and cranberries.

VEGAN, PALEO, GF, RAW MAKES 10 WRAPS

Sauce:

1 cup tamarind paste (no sugar added)

3 tablespoons maple syrup

1 tablespoon coconut aminos

1 tablespoon coconut oil

Pinch of sea salt

Wraps:

5 large collard green leaves

2 carrots

1 cucumber

½ large mango

1 avocado

10 teaspoons raw almond butter

Cilantro

Start by making the sauce. Simply stir all the sauce ingredients together and then set it aside.

Wash the collard greens and pat them dry. Carefully cut out the stem and continue cutting to halve the leaf. One half leaf makes one wrap.

Cut the carrots, cucumber, and mango julienne style, in thin, long strips. Cut the avocado in half and slice that into thin strips, too.

To assemble, place the collard green leaf bright side down and smear 1 teaspoon almond butter toward one edge, leaving enough leaf on the side to allow you to fold it over the filling. Place a few strips of each ingredient on top of the almond butter, sprinkle with a few cilantro leaves, and drizzle with the tamarind sauce. Fold the leaf over and roll it until you have your wrap.

Place it fold side down on a serving plate. Repeat with the remaining wraps.

Serve with a bowl of tamarind sauce for dipping.

✳ TAMARIND BOOSTER

Tamarind is a fruit commonly used in Southeast Asian cooking. It has a slightly sweet, tart, and unique flavor that lends itself perfectly to dips and chutneys. It's loaded with fiber, and the fruit is commonly used in its native countries to battle constipation. It's also rich in minerals and B Vitamins.

summer rolls with un-peanut sauce

These are not greasy, deep-fried spring rolls but rather the soft, fresh, and incredibly delicious kind, loaded with healthy vegetables and a taste sensation of a dipping sauce. I love making this as a light lunch or dinner on a hot summer day. No need to switch the oven on!

VEGAN, GF MAKES 6 ROLLS

Un-Peanut Sauce:

- 2 tablespoons tahini
- Juice of ½ lime
- 1 tablespoon water
- 1 tablespoon almond or sunflower seed butter
- 1 inch ginger, grated
- 1 clove garlic, grated or finely chopped
- ½ teaspoon maple or coconut syrup
- 2 tablespoons coconut aminos (or hoisin sauce)
- ⅛ teaspoon sea salt
- ¼ teaspoon toasted sesame oil

To make the sauce, add the tahini, lime juice, and water to a bowl and stir well until it's all combined. Then add in the rest of the ingredients and mix well until you have a thick, smooth sauce. Taste to determine whether you need more salt or maple syrup. Set aside when finished.

Rolls:

2 cups brown rice vermicelli noodles

6 brown rice spring roll wrappers (or white rice ones)

1 avocado, sliced

18 mint leaves

18 leaves Thai basil (or regular basil)

⅓ cup cilantro leaves

2 carrots, julienned

½ head Boston lettuce (about 6 large leaves), washed and dried

Prepare all your roll ingredients. Boil the rice noodles according to the package description. They should need to boil only about 1–2 minutes. Then rinse under cold water to cool.

For the rice paper, prepare a big bowl of hot water and cover a cutting board with a clean, damp kitchen towel. To assemble, dip the rice paper in the hot water and place on the damp towel. Place two slices of avocado horizontally in the middle of the round rice paper. Place three leaves each of mint and basil and a sprig of cilantro on top, then a small pile of carrots, lettuce and noodles. Fold in the sides, left and right, and then fold the bottom part over your filling and continue rolling until you have a tight wrap. The paper should stick together easily, and that means once you roll, you can't go back. Be careful not to overstuff the wraps.

Serve the wraps with individual bowls of dipping sauce. That way people can double dip as they wish!

✳ TAHINI/SESAME BOOSTER

Sesame seeds might be small, but they are jam-packed with protein, fiber, and healthy fats. They have long been used to relieve constipation; and because each seed is 50 percent oil, they help lubricate the intestines. Sesame is also a great source of calcium.

cabbage rolls
with shrimp

In this dish sushi meets cabbage roll in a fun, festive, and flavor-packed package. These are great to bring along for lunch or as an addition to a potluck. Or make them all just for you!

GF MAKES 6 ROLLS

1½ cups brown rice (or any rice you like), cooked and cooled

1 tablespoon lime juice

1 tablespoon rice vinegar

1 tablespoon honey

½ chili, minced and seeds removed, OR ¼ teaspoon dried chili flakes

¼ teaspoon sea salt

6 large, perfect savoy cabbage leaves

2 tablespoons coconut oil

12 shrimp, peeled, tails on

1 tablespoon finely minced ginger

1 cup yellow pepper, sliced

1 cup red pepper, sliced

1 teaspoon sea salt

Tamari, coconut aminos, or a sweet chili sauce for serving

In a bowl, mix together the lime juice, vinegar, honey, chili, and salt. Drizzle over the room temperature rice and combine well. Set aside.

Bring a large pot of water to a boil. Cut away the thickest part of the cabbage stems and drop the leaves into the boiling water. Leave them in for about 30 seconds or until the leaves have softened and still look bright. Remove the leaves and let them cool and dry on a paper towel.

Add 2 tablespoons coconut oil to a medium-hot pan. Add the shrimp, ginger, and peppers to the pan.

To assemble, place a spoonful of rice at the bottom part of a leaf and press it down. Add two shrimps and some peppers. Fold in the sides and roll up from the bottom. Be careful not to overstuff or roll it too tight—the leaf might break.

Serve with a small bowl of tamari, coconut aminos, or a sweet chili sauce.

zucchini "pasta" with pesto

This is a light, summery take on pasta with pesto. Zucchini is especially delicious in the summer months, and its shape and consistency make it a great grain-free and gluten-free alternative to pasta. It's delicious on its own or served with some grilled fish or chicken.

Leftover pesto will last three or four days in the fridge. It's great as a dip for crudités, thinned with more oil or water as a salad dressing, or drizzled over steamed or roasted vegetables.

VEGAN, PALEO, GF, RAW SERVES 2

1 cup raw, shelled pistachios

½ cup water

½ teaspoon salt

1 cup pea shoots (or spinach)

1 tablespoon lemon juice

Freshly ground pepper

2 zucchini, sliced thin or in thin spirals using a spiral slicer

Freshly grated Parmesan (optional)

Add all the ingredients, except the olive oil and the zucchini, to a blender or food processor. Start the blender and slowly drizzle in the olive oil. Once smooth, stop the blender and taste. Add more salt, pepper, or lemon juice if needed.

To serve, add about 5 tablespoons of pesto to the zucchini and mix.

Add a generous sprinkle of freshly grated Parmesan if desired, for a little more oomph.

✳ PISTACHIO BOOSTER

The bright green pistachio is a great source of minerals—especially copper and the calming mineral magnesium. They are anti-inflammatory and contain healthy fats. Interestingly, folk medicine has long used pistachios to combat jaundice, and more recent studies seem to support that use. I love it when we find proof that food really is medicine.

green frittata

This dish is great for a big brunch with friends or family and a great contribution to a potluck or picnic. It's delicious hot or cold and will keep stored in the fridge for a couple of days.

VEGETARIAN SERVES 8

8 eggs

1 tablespoon butter

2 cloves garlic, chopped fine

½ leek, washed and chopped

1 small zucchini, cubed

3 cups spinach, washed

1 sprig fresh oregano, roughly chopped, OR 1 teaspoon dried oregano or Italian herb blend

¼ teaspoon salt

Freshly ground pepper

¾ cup crumbled sheep's milk feta cheese

Preheat the oven to 350°F. Crack all the eggs into a bowl and beat them together lightly.

In a large, medium-hot pan, melt the butter and add the garlic. Sauté for 1 minute; then add the leek. Sauté for another 3 minutes, until the leek is soft; then add the zucchini and sauté for another 2 minutes, stirring often.

Add the spinach and let it wilt, adding in more once there's space in the pan. Finally, add in the oregano, salt, and pepper and stir.

If you make this in a cast-iron skillet, just switch the heat off, pour the eggs over the vegetables, sprinkle in the feta cheese, and pop the whole thing into the oven.

Otherwise, add all the vegetables to a large pie pan or baking dish. You could also make little individual pies using a muffin pan. Just remember to leave room for the eggs to rise. Pour the beaten eggs over the vegetables, add the crumbled feta cheese, and stir gently to make sure the vegetables and cheese are distributed evenly.

Bake for 35–45 minutes. The frittata is done when a knife inserted into the middle of it comes out clean. Let it rest for 10 minutes before cutting into it. Serve with a big green salad and some crackers or bread and grass-fed butter.

EGG BOOSTER

The incredible egg is so much more than just a great and affordable source of protein. The egg yolk is rich in choline, an important component for proper brain function and overall health. Quality really matters when it comes to choosing the right eggs—so go the extra mile and get eggs from hens that are outdoors and eat a varied diet (that is, pastured). Such eggs are a great source of vitamin D and omega-3s.

gluten-free pasta with greens and mushroom sauté

Pasta is such a staple dish and an easy go-to when you need a satisfying, crowd-pleasing dinner on the table fast. I love that you can easily customize it with whatever you have on hand, what's in season, or what you crave that day. This combination is grounding, earthy, and fall-ish, with beans, mushrooms, and kale.

GF SERVES 2

1 tablespoon olive oil

2 cloves garlic, minced

1 small yellow onion, chopped

2 cups sliced mushrooms of your choice

1 cup broccoli florets

2 cups chopped kale

1 cup precooked or canned adzuki beans (any other beans would work, too)

1 small can anchovy filets, chopped fine

1 cup uncooked brown rice pasta or quinoa pasta (penne or fusilli)

¼ cup chopped fresh basil

Heat a deep pan or skillet, add the olive oil and minced garlic. Sauté for 1 minute, being careful not to burn the garlic. If that happens, start over—burned garlic does not taste good.

Add the chopped onion and sauté for about 5 minutes, until the onion turns translucent and soft. Add the mushrooms and broccoli, and sauté for another few minutes. Toss in the kale, cooked beans, and anchovies.

Cook the pasta according to the package instructions. Drain, saving about ⅓ cup of starchy cooking water. Finally, toss the pasta and the sautéed vegetables together and add a splash of the cooking water. Combine everything well.

Just before serving, add the basil.

a bowl full of goodness

I wish this was my invention, but it's definitely not. You might have seen similar dishes before, often referred to as Buddha Bowl, Grain Bowl, Macrobiotic Bowl, and others. It is a tried and trusted favorite for a reason; the combinations and possibilities are endless. So some ideas are presented below, but go ahead and use your favorite grains, your favorite greens, beans, and vegetables and make the combination that is just right for you.

I recommend soaking all grains for eight hours before cooking to remove antinutrients and make the grains more digestible. It even makes the cooking time shorter.

VEGAN, GF SERVES 2

Sauce:

2 garlic cloves, smashed

1 inch fresh ginger, grated

1 tablespoon almond butter

¼ cup whole almonds (preferably soaked)

Juice of ½ lemon

1 tablespoon tamari

1 tablespoon water

¼ cup fresh cilantro

Pinch of cayenne pepper

Splash of water if needed

Grains:

½ cup quinoa

1 cup pure water

¼ teaspoon sea salt

Kombu (optional)

Veggies:

½ kabocha squash

2 carrots, sliced

½ large daikon radish, sliced

1 leek, sliced

½ cup broccoli florets

Handful sugar snap peas

½ bunch kale, stem removed, torn into chunks

Garnish:

1 tablespoon dulse

1 tablespoon chopped cilantro

1 tablespoon raw sauerkraut or kimchi

To make the sauce, place all the sauce ingredients in a blender or food processor and blend well. Then set aside. (If you don't have a blender, you can omit the whole almonds and mix all the other sauce ingredients together in a bowl and stir well.)

Rinse the quinoa well, multiple times, until no "foam" omit the whole almonds and mix appears in the sieve. Add the quinoa, water, salt, and kombu (if using) to a pot and cook for 20 minutes or until water is evaporated. Test the quinoa. Omit the whole almonds and mix if it's still too crunchy, add a splash of water and cook for another 3 minutes or until done.

While the quinoa cooks, add 1 cup of water to a pot and place a steam basket in the pot. Layer your vegetables in the basket with the harder vegetables such as squash and carrots first and the rest on top, with the kale last. Put the lid on and steam until tender but not mushy.

To build your bowl, layer a cup of cooked quinoa at the bottom of a serving bowl. Place the vegetables on top, keeping each vegetable "grouped" together, laid down side by side. Pour the sauce on top and sprinkle with some dulse and freshly chopped cilantro. Omit the whole almonds and mix and for a digestive aid, add a tablespoon of raw sauerkraut or kimchi on top.

spring comfort pasta

Spring vegetables really get to shine in a simple pasta dish like this. I've made it gluten free by simply using gluten free pasta here. You could even make it paleo by using zucchini noodles instead, or any other pasta variety you like.

GF SERVES 4

4 servings rice pasta or quinoa pasta (about 8 oz dried pasta)

¾ cup pine nuts

1 small bunch broccoli or 1½ cups broccoli florets, cut into bite-size bouquets

1 zucchini, halved and sliced

¾ cup green peas (frozen is fine)

2 cups chopped spinach or kale

2 scallions or spring onions, chopped

2 cups cooked chicken or 2 chicken breasts

2 or more tablespoons dandelion pesto (recipe on page 155)

Salt and pepper

Bring big pot of water to a boil for the pasta. In the meantime, warm a pan to medium heat and add the pine nuts. Stir the nuts a couple of times and remove from the heat once they are fragrant and golden. Set aside.

Add salt to the pasta water and add the pasta. Stir and cook for almost all its cooking time. When there's 2 minutes left of the cooking time, add in the broccoli, zucchini, and peas. Cook for 2 minutes and add the spinach last. Drain the pasta and vegetables and add them back to the pot.

If you are cooking chicken breasts from scratch, cut the breasts into 1-inch slices, sprinkle with a little salt and pepper, and cook in a frying pan over medium heat with 1 tablespoon olive oil. If you are using leftover cooked chicken, just gently warm the chicken in a pan over low heat with 1 teaspoon olive oil.

Add the warm, cooked chicken to your pasta mix. Stir in 2 generous spoonfuls of dandelion pesto. Sprinkle on the pine nuts and serve.

treats

Let's not forget about the most important part of the meal: desserts and treats! I believe that we should treat ourselves every day, but with nourishing and truly delicious real food. So skip the processed junk and try something from this chapter instead. And who knows? You might just end up liking it better than that three p.m. candy bar.

green lemon sorbet

Have you ever tried making your own sorbet? It's easier than you think and totally delicious. The only equipment you need is a blender. The best part is that you can skip all the added sugar and instead use fresh, whole fruit and a splash of honey. I love it.

VEGAN, PALEO, GF, SUGAR FREE SERVES 2

1 banana

½ lemon with seeds and peel but thick rind on end cut off

1 packed cup raw baby spinach

¼ avocado, peeled

1 tablespoon liquid raw honey

½ cup ice

Mint sprig for garnish

Add all the ingredients except the mint to a blender. (A powerful processor might get the job done, too.) Blend until everything is well combined into a soft-serve kind of texture.

Scoop a dollop of the mixture into an emptied half lemon and serve with a little mint sprig as garnish.

green smoothie

Okay, since I already wrote a whole book on green smoothies and juices called Best Green Drinks Ever, I won't go on about the benefits and deliciousness of these drinks. Let me just say that I'm a fan, and this one is a winner, for breakfast, lunch, a snack, or even dessert. Because it's that good.

VEGAN, PALEO, GF, SUGAR FREE SERVES 1

½ cup full-fat coconut milk

½ cup coconut water

1 packed cup chopped kale

1 frozen banana

1 tablespoon hemp seeds

1 teaspoon chia or flax seeds

½ teaspoon vanilla

Add all the ingredients to a blender and blend well.
Serve with a straw and sip slow.

beets and greens juice

Here's another easy way for you to use up a whole bunch of beets: make juice. I like to think of vegetable and green juices as my instant multivitamin pills. The nutrients get absorbed into the bloodstream quickly, and you'll feel a nice boost of vitality and energy.

VEGAN, PALEO, GF, SUGAR FREE SERVES 1

½ orange

½ lemon

1 inch ginger

2 stalks celery

2 beets

2 cups roughly chopped beet greens

½ cucumber

1 apple

Wash and chop all the vegetables to fit your juicer's size requirement.

Run all the fruits and vegetables through the juicer, placing some leafy greens in between harder fruits like apple and cucumber.

Drink right away.

✳ BEETROOT BOOSTER

This beautiful pink root is a great source of folic acid and fiber. The compound that gives beets that deep pink color (betacyanin) is a powerful anticancer agent. Beets also have a stimulating, boosting effect on the liver's detoxing process, and all that healthy fiber is great for digestion and managing cholesterol levels. This is one beautiful, powerful food we should all be eating a lot of. The greens are rich in minerals, inculdong folic acid and iron, and are totally delicious cooked, raw or in a juice.

green smoothie breakfast bowl

This is basically a thicker, colder take on a green smoothie—served in a bowl and eaten with a spoon. It's a great breakfast or snack anytime, fun to eat, absolutely delicious, and oh so nutritious. Take that, cereal.

For topping options, try shredded coconut, chia seeds, hemp seeds, nuts, cocoa nibs, granola, raw oats, berries, mango . . . or whatever else you fancy.

VEGAN, PALEO, GF, SUGAR FREE SERVES 2

1 cup coconut water

1 tablespoon chia seeds

1 frozen banana

½ cup frozen mango chunks

¼ cup cilantro, chopped

1 cup chopped kale

¼ avocado

1 table spoon coconut oil

Juice of ½ lime

Add all the ingredients to a blender. Blend, starting on slow speed and slowly increasing it. Blend until thick and smooth. Pour mixture into a cereal bowl and sprinkle with any and all of your chosen toppings.

frozen green juice popsicles

That's right. I basically just froze some green juice, and—voilà—a cold, yummy, and healthy treat on a hot summer day. Sugar free and loaded with antioxidants and greens for glowing skin and sun protection from the inside out.

You can make your own popsicle molds with a wooden or plastic spoon stuck into a freezer-proof glass jar or plastic or paper cup.

VEGAN, PALEO, GF, SUGAR FREE MAKES 3–4, DEPENDING ON SIZE OF MOLDS

1 cucumber

1 mango

Juice of ½ lime

10 mint leaves

1 cup packed baby kale or baby spinach

Run all the ingredients through a juicer. Pour the juice into popsicle molds and freeze for at least 6 hours.

To remove, gently rinse the mold under warm water until you are able to slide the popsicles out.

MANGO BOOSTER

Mangoes are rich in enzymes that help aid in proper digestion and are a great source of antioxidants, vitamins A and C, and iron. The carotenoids found in this tropical fruit are wonderful for protecting us from cancer and promoting healthy-looking skin.

peachy popsicles

These cold pops taste like delicious peachy iced tea. They are loaded with fresh fruits, greens and antioxidant-loaded green tea. It's the perfect treat when you need a cold pick-me-up.

VEGAN, PALEO, GF, SUGAR FREE MAKES 3–4, DEPENDING ON SIZE OF MOLDS

2 peaches

1 inch ginger

½ lime

5 leaves romaine or Boston lettuce

1 sprig basil

½ cup iced green tea

1 tablespoon maple syrup

Run all the ingredients, except the iced tea and maple syrup, through a juicer. Then stir in the iced tea and maple syrup.

Pour the mixture into popsicle molds and freeze for at least 6 hours.

To remove, gently rinse the mold under warm water until you are able to slide the popsicles out of the molds.

green and creamy popsicles

Yes – you can have ice cream even if you don't eat dairy! Coconuts to the rescue! The rich, creamy and sweet coconut milk is perfect for using in popsicles, fudgesicles and ice cream. It's loaded with satisfying and weight-loss boosting fatty acids and the mint has cooling benefits, perfect for hot summer nights.

VEGAN, PALEO, GF, SUGAR FREE MAKES 6

1 13.5 fl oz can coconut milk

2 packed cups spinach

1 mango or 1 cup frozen mango

10 mint leaves

2 tablespoons raw honey

Blend all the ingredients in a blender or food processor. Make sure to get them completely smooth. Pour the liquid into popsicle molds.

Stick in the freezer and let sit for at least 6 hours, or until the popsicles are completely frozen.

To remove, gently rinse the mold under hot water and slide the popsicles out of the mold.

✳ COCONUT MILK BOOSTER

This luscious, creamy milk is loaded with good-for-you, medium-chain fatty acids. Fifty percent of the saturated fats in coconut are in the form of medium-chain fatty acids (also called lauric acids), which have antiviral and antibacterial properties that help protect us from disease. These fats are also very easily absorbed and actually preferred as an energy source by the body, rather than just stored as fat. And, most impressive of all, burning these fats for energy increases metabolic rate, which means that more calories are burned. So if you're looking to lose weight, eat coconut in any form. It's also rich in minerals.

greenola

What is this exactly? Think grain-free "granola" with seeds, nuts, and—you guessed it—greens! Genius, if I do say so myself. This is a great portable snack to eat as is. It's also delicious with some berries and fresh almond milk or on top of full-fat yogurt, kefir, or coconut yogurt.

VEGAN (IF USING OTHER MENTIONED SYRUPS,) PALEO, GF MAKES 5-6 CUPS

2 cups kale, measured with stems removed, leaves torn into small pieces

2 Medjool dates, chopped

2 cups coconut flakes

⅓ cup goji berries (or dried cranberries or raisins)

¾ cup chopped walnuts

¾ cup pumpkin seeds

2 tablespoons chia seeds

3 tablespoons coconut oil

2 tablespoons raw honey (or coconut syrup, brown rice syrup, or maple syrup)

¼ teaspoon sea salt

Preheat the oven to 250°F and line a baking sheet with parchment paper.

Add all the ingredients to a bowl and mix well. Make sure the honey and coconut are evenly distributed. Spread the mixture onto the baking sheet. Place in the oven.

Bake for 10 minutes, take it out and toss the ingredients. Bake for another 10–15 minutes, or until the mixture is golden and the kale is crispy.

Take it out and let it cool completely before placing in an airtight container.

✳ PUMPKIN SEED BOOSTER

So many of us don't eat enough zinc—a mineral that is important for a properly functioning immune system and promotes normal growth and development, and pumpkin seeds happen to be a great source of this vital mineral. Pumpkin seeds have also been found to be very beneficial for prostate health.

zucchini
chocolate squares

I don't really think "hiding" vegetables in delicious foods is necessary, although it might seem like that's what's going on here. Nevertheless, people are going to love these, and they won't even know they're eating good-for-you vegetables, seeds, and nuts—because it's all coated in chocolate. Brilliant!

If you're making this for kids or for adults with a sweet tooth, you might want to add two extra tablespoons honey for extra sweetness.

1 tablespoon ground flax seed

3 tablespoons water (or 1 egg)

½ cup almond flour

1 teaspoon baking soda

1 teaspoon cinnamon

¼ teaspoon nutmeg

2 tablespoons cocoa powder

1 tablespoon chia seeds

⅛ teaspoon salt

½ cup almond butter

¼ cup coconut oil

1 teaspoon vanilla

⅓ cup raw honey

1½ cups grated zucchini (press with paper towel before measuring to remove excess water)

½ cup chopped hazelnuts

⅓ cup currants or raisins

¼ cup dark chocolate chips (optional)

Preheat the oven to 350°F. Stir together the flax seed and water and set aside for 10–15 minutes.

Meanwhile, combine all the dry ingredients (through salt in the list of ingredients) in a bowl and mix well. Add the wet ingredients and flax seed mixture (through honey) to the dry and mix everything together. Then fold in the zucchini, hazelnuts, currants or raisins, and chocolate chips if using.

Line a 9 × 9 baking pan with parchment paper and pour the mixture into the pan.

Bake for 20–30 minutes, or until a toothpick inserted into the middle comes out clean.

Remove from the oven and let rest for 10 minutes (this is truly the hardest part of the whole baking process) and cut into squares.

ALMOND BOOSTER

Almonds are the most nutrient-dense nuts of them all and have a high fiber and protein content. They are a good source of calcium and magnesium and healthy fats that can help lower cholesterol. And did you know almonds contain pain-blocking compounds? Try a few next time you have a headache!

zucchini kale muffins

This recipe is for all you cheddar scone lovers out there. These are a delicious savory snack option, a perfect pastry or bread alternative, and they're great alongside alight soup or salad.

VEGAN, PALEO, GF MAKES 12 LARGE MUFFINS OR 24 SMALL ONES

1 tablespoon chia seeds

1 tablespoon ground flax seeds

6 tablespoons water

2 cups almond flour

⅛ teaspoon freshly ground pepper

5 tablespoons nutritional yeast (you can also add some grated cheddar or Parmesan)

1 teaspoon baking soda

½ teaspoon salt

¼ teaspoon nutmeg

⅓ cup coconut oil, melted

1 tablespoon lemon juice

1 cup grated zucchini

1 cup kale, measured with stems removed and leaves chopped fine

4 tablespoons canned coconut milk

Preheat the oven to 400°F and grease 12 muffin tins.

Mix the chia and flax seeds with the water and set aside for 15 minutes to let the mixture thicken.

Meanwhile, add all the dry ingredients to a bowl and mix well. Add the coconut oil, lemon juice, and the seed mix and stir well. Then add in the zucchini and kale and as much coconut milk as needed to make a batter (it should be a thick batter).

Place the batter in the muffin tins and place the pan in the oven. Bake for 15 minutes (or more if needed). Test the muffins by sticking a toothpick into the middle—if it comes out dry, the muffins are done. Enjoy!

INDEX

ACKNOWLEDGEMENTS

I want to thank Ann Treistman from The Countryman Press for her continued trust in me and for her enthusiasm and passion for sharing healthy lifestyle, food and cooking tips with the world. Thanks for giving me a chance, again! A big thanks to the whole team at Countryman Press and the graphic designer who brought all of my notes and images to life.

A BIG thank you to my awesome husband for always believing in me, for being an amazing baby daddy to our little Felix and for giving me the time, space and free hands I needed to cook up all these dishes! Thanks to my little man Felix for playing along patiently and for taste testing all of Mamma's food. You are my everything.

Thanks to my own mamma, Anne Lise, for installing in me an appreciation for real, fuss-free and delicious home cooked food! Thanks to my super-grandmothers who both managed to raise kids and work to provide for their families while putting dinner on the table every night. I don't know how they did it all. And thanks to my whole family in Norway, who always gather around home-cooked food for some quality time.

Thanks to the Institute for Integrative Nutrition, where I got my health coaching degree, for continuing to push the boundaries and empowering me to go out and actually do what I want to do.

Thanks to Patryce Bak for all the beautiful photographs and for keeping up with the bootcamp-style photoshoot weekend we had in the middle of summer.

A big thank you to Dr. Frank Lipman for being a beacon of knowledge and yet continuing to stay curious and generous in sharing his passion and wisdom. I am honored to work along side him and the rest of the team at the Eleven Eleven Wellness Center.

Thanks to my foodie friends for continuing to challenge my palate and for making me strive to cook food that is not just healthy and good for you, but also incredibly delicious.